PLAYS FROM VAULT 4

3 BILLION SECONDS
Maud Dromgoole

ALCATRAZ
Nathan Lucky Wood

COLLAPSIBLE
Margaret Perry

INSIDE VOICES
Nabilah Said

JERICHO
MALAPROP Theatre

OPEN
Christopher Adams & Timothy Allsop

THROWN
Jodi Gray

PLAYS FROM VAULT 4

3 BILLION SECONDS
Maud Dromgoole

ALCATRAZ
Nathan Lucky Wood

COLLAPSIBLE
Margaret Perry

INSIDE VOICES
Nabilah Said

JERICHO
MALAPROP Theatre

OPEN
Christopher Adams & Timothy Allsop

THROWN
Jodi Gray

NICK HERN BOOKS
London
www.nickhernbooks.co.uk

A Nick Hern Book

Plays from VAULT 4 first published in Great Britain in 2019 as a paperback original by Nick Hern Books Limited, The Glasshouse, 49a Goldhawk Road, London W12 8QP, in association with VAULT Festival

Cover image by Thomas Kirk Shannon, VAULT Festival Designer & Art Director

Designed and typeset by Nick Hern Books, London
Printed and bound in Great Britain by Mimeo Ltd, Huntingdon, Cambridgeshire PE29 6XX

A CIP catalogue record for this book is available from the British Library

ISBN 978 1 84842 823 2

Contents

Welcome to VAULT   vii

3 Billion Seconds by Maud Dromgoole   1

Alcatraz by Nathan Lucky Wood   85

Collapsible by Margaret Perry   139

Inside Voices by Nabilah Said   185

JERICHO by MALAPROP Theatre   229

Open by Christopher Adams & Timothy Allsop   263

Thrown by Jodi Gray   323

Welcome to VAULT

The magic of the theatre often lies in its transience. There's something special in the live event, in the shared space of bodies crammed into a room to witness a good story well told. Imagine that, multiplied by ten, and you've got the inarticulable atmosphere of VAULT Festival – dozens of stories unfolding in one moment to thousands of captive audience members. It is theatre at its most vibrant, its most immediate, its most live.

Plays though – what makes them special is the way that they live on long after the stage goes dark. For writers, seeing their script published represents a permanent life for their work. It allows the stories they've dreamed up to reach out to people long after their run with us has ended. Publishing a script preserves, but it also reinvigorates – placing the story firmly into the imaginations of new readers and audience members and artists for years and years to come.

This year, VAULT Festival is honoured to welcome one of its strongest contingents of new writing yet. The emerging artists that we work with are bursting at the seams with stories, ranging from elaborate escape plans to playful ruminations on the state of the world, from measuring the value of a single life to celebrating the warmth of a community.

The writers and stories chosen here represent a small portion of the talent on offer from the VAULT Festival family. Our artists are teeming with love and intelligence and rage, they are brimming with urgency and voice and soul and ready to tear up the stage. As far as we're concerned, they are the writers, makers and tellers of the future, and now, their stories are in your hands.

As always, none of this would be possible without the unwavering support of Nick Hern Books. Their dedicated belief in our artists and consistent investment in their talent is essential to our work. From the bottom of our hearts, thank you.

Gillian Greer, Head of Theatre and Performance
VAULT Festival 2019

This book went to press before the end of rehearsals and so the texts may differ slightly from the plays as performed.

3 BILLION SECONDS

Maud Dromgoole

*For Jessica,
who against all good maths
brought me into the world*

MAUD DROMGOOLE

Maud Dromgoole is a writer from London. Her plays include *Mary's Babies* (VAULT Festival/King's Head/Fertility Fest @ Bush Theatre/Jermyn Street Theatre); *Rosa, Ursula and Richard* (Finalist Mercury Weinberger Prize; reading at Old Red Lion); *Blue Moon* (Bread and Roses/The Courtyard/Arcola – as short play). Her short plays include *Sleeping Beauty* (The Bunker); *Milk* (The Bunker/Hackney Attic); *Cake* (The Cockpit/Tristan Bates Theatre); *The Boy James* (Love Bites); *A Violet in the Youth of Primy Nature* (Theatre Utopia) and *Selkie* (Southwark Playhouse/Old Red Lion). Her sitcom *Acting Up* was shortlisted for BBC Writersroom Comedy Script Room and she is currently working on several short films.

3 Billion Seconds was first performed at VAULT Festival, London, on 6 March 2019, directed by Beth Pitts.

At the time of going to print the play was still to be cast.

A previous, shorter version of the play was performed at The Miniaturists, Arcola Theatre, London, with the following cast:

DAISY   Rhiannon Neads
MICHAEL   Tayla Kovacevic-Ebong

3 Billion Seconds was started on an Arvon course under the tutorage of Chris Thorpe and Alice Birch, both of whom have been incredibly generous with their time and ideas. As has the excellent Beth Pitts.

Thanks to Gill Greer and everyone at VAULT. Thanks to everyone at Nick Hern Books.

Huge thanks are owed to my Playgroup: Joel McCormack, Max Levine, Sonia Jalaly, Hatty Jones and especially to Jessica Dromgoole, Jenny Bakst and Margaret Perry who have each seen this play through many drafts, tantrums, and panicky phone calls.

Thanks to my supportive family, especially Cat Horn, Gordon Snell, Agnes Dromgoole, Matilda James and Chris Morgan. Thanks also to Greg Kyle, Jodi Gray, Natasha Magigi, Felicity Thompson, Grizzie Elliot, Laura Horton, Celia De Wolff and Olivia Ross.

Thanks to James and Izzi at The Miniaturists for giving me some space to try this play, to Eleanor and Sophie for helping it run smoothly, and Tayla and Rhiannon for giving it breath.

M.D.

One simply feels convinced that someone – the government or God – will somehow stop it, before it disturbs our comfortable and settled lives... It takes a long time to realise that as far as looking after the future of humankind and the earth is concerned, there is no one at the controls.

John Davol

The power of population is so superior to the power of the Earth to produce subsistence for man, that premature death must in some shape or other visit the human race.

Thomas Malthus

Note on Play

The first word has been underlined to indicate a break of space, time or character. Characters have not been distinguished but should be obvious.

Words in [square brackets] are unspoken.

A forward slash (/) indicates an interruption, including self-interruption.

A lack of full stop indicates an open-endedness.

The world that is of interest to the characters contracts as the play progresses and this should be represented somehow physically.

Their relationship with the audience is inversely related to their relationship with each other.

The audience begins as their allies but, as they become more intimate and insular with each other, we lose them.

We are moving outwards to inwards.

We are becoming more compact.

There is a lot of love.

A clock is visible on stage showing Earth's current population. An example can be found here: www.worldometers.info/world-population

DAISY	MICHAEL
We are a plague on earth.	
	When I was born.
1990	
	Yep. Thanks.
Good year.	
	The population stood at just over five billion.
Five point two.	
	Five point two nine six actually
Five point two nine six and one.	
She cheesily winks at him and points.	
	By the time I was twenty.
The population had increased	
Drum roll	
	By thirty per cent.
That's loads.	
	In my grandfather's lifetime
Between 1900 and 2000	
	The increase in world population was
Three. Times. Greater.	
	Than during the entire previous history of humanity.
Going from one point six	
	To six point one
Billion people	
	In just over three billion seconds.

Michael and I

Met on stage

Population Pow wow

Coventry

2016

And from the second I saw her

Hell did we hate each other.

Michael was a paralegal with a degree in superiority.

Daisy was a 'Poet'

Don't do the air quotes.

Daisy was a poet '…'

We had 'undeniable chemistry on stage'

And unbelievable rows offstage.

But it sort of…

Worked.

We launched a small Kickstarter

Funded almost exclusively by Daisy's estranged
wealthy pare[nts] /

And toured any conference centre,

Student Union

Or village hall who would have us.

It was hell.

Michael was attempting a vegan hygiene regime and smelt
vaguely of kettle chips.

MICHAEL *counts out on his fingers.*

Daisy spent a week

Of both of our lives speaking

Only in haiku

We didn't care for each other

        But we both cared a lot about /

<u>Population</u> is the single greatest threat to humanity

        But we can change that.

Simply educating men and women about population can have
a huge impact.

    When Iran introduced a national family-planning programme

1989

        Its fertility rate fell from five point six births per woman

To two point six.

             In a decade.

        <u>We</u> shared a lot of cheap B&B rooms.

And stayed up late drinking conference-centre wine out of
plastic cups.

        Putting the world to rights.

<u>King</u> of the world for the next thirty seconds.

               K

Go

Solve the NHS

        Scrap private health care

Solve education

        Scrap private schools

Solve immigration

        Scrap borders

Solve wealth distribution

        Scrap inheritance

Feed the world

        Scrap

                                    Eating

                              So much meat.

Solve population.

                        Scrap having babies.

Solve ageing population.

                                     Scrap

Out of Time

                            Treating cancer?

That's a lot of scrapping for thirty seconds.

                          I'm very scrappy.

When it comes to the three 'F' words.

                                      Fuel.

Food.

                          And Fresh water.

We are

                                    Fucked

Fucked

                            And Fucked.

And we are getting more fucked.

                        The more fucking

People are doing.

                  We didn't get huge audiences.

Which, given we were acutely aware of how many people there
were in the world

                  Was quite disheartening.

But we kept each other's spirits up.

                              If you had to,

                                 had to,

                          kill someone,

anyone in the world,

who would it be and how would you do it?

Donald Trump.

Wholly unoriginal and wholly unfeasible.

I'm very wily.

How would you do it?

Hit him.

Very 'wily'.

With a newspaper.

Very. Ironic.

Seriously, try it. Don't try it. But seriously.

Take like, twenty-three sheets.

'Like' twenty-three sheets?

Well twenty-two's not strong enough, twenty-four's not malleable enough.

Okay.

So right take twenty-three sheets.

Slide them apart by... three inches, roll it up,

Fold it in the middle,

Smash anything you wanna break with it.

Right.

And it's environmentally friendly. How many murder weapons can you think of that are both recycled and recyclable.

Ice?

We'd get drunk.

And had heavy-headed mornings.

But whatever happened.

We'd always make it

To Breakfast.

We had a similar sense of value

And budget

And

Whatever happened.

We'd sit together.

And try and reach our daily calorie allowance by 10 a.m.

<u>Eggs</u>

Fried

Two

Two hundred and eight calories

Sausages

Three

Four hundred and eighty-six calories

Baked Beans

Half tin

One hundred and forty calories

Fried bread

Two

One hundred and eighty-two Calories

Fried mushrooms

Portion

One hundred and fifty-six calories

Hash brown

Three

Two hundred and forty Calories

Grilled Tomato.

One

Sixty-four Calories

Toast

White.

Buttered.

Two

Slices.

Two hundred and fifty Calories.

Black Pudding.

If we were lucky.

Two slices.

One hundred and ninety calories.

Ketchup

One tablespoon

Twenty calories.

Brown sauce

One tablespoon

Twenty calories.

Combining.

To make a grand total of.

One thousand nine hundred and fifty-six Calories.

Leaving a spare forty-four calories.

For a small coffee.

With a splash of milk.

And three teaspoons of sugar.

We liked the maths.

And gradually.

Very gradually.

We fell in

To a routine of semi-regular sex.

Which was good.

It was actually really great.

During China's One-Child Policy

Fertility fell from six births per woman in the 1960s

To one point five in 2014.

Though of course their methods were highly controversial.

Effective.

Autocratic. And.

Sadly.

CanNot be replicated in other countries.

But

Women hold the /

This here is my hospital letter.

Access to proper medical care including abortion /

Tomorrow.

I am taking matters into my own hands.

Into my own balls.

From tomorrow, all I can say is, if you like your grapes seedless.

What the fuck was that?

What. I was flirting with the audience.

You

Completely overrode my female-empowerment argument,

With your vain,

Self-serving,

Vasectomy bullshit.

Hey now, I'm just trying to remove the vas deferens between us.

Daisy hates puns.

Daisy hates puns almost as much as she hates it when I forget about female empowerment.

We had a whole new bit on the Campaign for
Women and Girls.

I'm sorry I forgot.

You forgot. Have you got early-onset...

Jack my er, dad does have Alzheimer's, which is why Daisy has trailed off.

I'm so sorry.

She never used to mention dementia before she knew, but there's a compulsive part of Daisy's brain that always makes her say the worst possible thing.

It's surprisingly useful.

It's fine.

It's not fine.

Don't worry. We'll both let it go.

Okay.

Jack's very not well.

I don't see him much.

He doesn't know who I am any more and the more time I spend with him the less I feel I have edges.

I accidentally let slip he lived in [place] when we were touring [place] and in a deliberate attempt to piss me off, Daisy went to say

Hello.

Doll.

Daisy, actually.

Dolly… my…

Dolly was a sweetheart of my father's who slipped off the side
of a waltzer car on a trip to Margate.

He held on to her hands but her body was mangled
in the motor.

She died a little too slowly.

Squeezing his hands. So tight.

They left scars.

He can't remember her real name, only her face, which he
mistakes for Daisy's.

I brought you a beeswax wrap.

Daisy found a new way to upset me.

You use it instead of cling film.

And Jack found his lost

Lovely pattern isn't it.

Can I hold your hands Dolly?

Not just now.

Maybe later.

Maybe later.

He gasps.

Ten past two!

Time for *Countdown*.

Is it? Is it time for *Countdown* Dolly?

I think we might just catch it.

I take the only tape from the shelf and put it into his
crumbling VHS player.

Nine hundred and fifteen.

Ten minus the one. Times one hundred. Seven plus the eight.

She's memorised the maths.

She hasn't memorised the maths.

I just can't do the maths.

How can eight point one seven four MILLION people
AFFORD to live in London.

Where the fuck is Plaistow?

Plaistow.

Where?

No you pronounce it. Plaistow.

I'm pretty sure you don't…

Our tour's coming to an end and our new favourite hobby is
fighting over digital listings.

One thousand two hundred and forty pounds.

It's a bit like Settlers of Catan

A month!

But less realistic.

How could it possibly be so expensive?

It has a wet room.

It has a shower over a toilet.

How does anyone afford to live on their own?

I think most people have friends.

And jobs.

That's a nice spreadsheet.

Thanks.

It has a sexy pie chart.

It has several sexy pie charts.

What's this bit?

Outgoings.

Nice. What's this bit?

Income.

−

Shit.

Yeah.

You can afford precisely half a flat.

Yep.

Perhaps if you agreed not to use the bathroom.

Just shat in the sink.

Yeah.

Yeah. Landlord would love that.

Went through all doorways sideways, using half the space.

Yeah. No good.

Or.

Yeah.

Or!

Yeah.

Just don't use the top half, cos you're actually
not that tall and if you found somewhere with
high ceilings or just like crouched a bit you could
get away with /

What?

No.

What?

No really it's nothing it's just not the or I thought
you were gonna say?

What 'or' did you want me to say?

No, I didn't want you to say it. I'd actually rather
live in a bin.

Than…?

<u>Me</u> and Michael move in together.

Ex-council block.

[Amount of money] plus bills.

Split between us.

It's a good deal.

It's a nice place.

It has shit water pressure.

It is south-facing.

It has blinds that we leave halfway open so that
we never have to actually open or close them.

It has IKEA furniture.

It is above a crack den.

It has a double lock.

We're not really together.

Other than the fact that we are together, all of the time.

Neither of us have ever been particularly happy.

And so adapt pretty well to living with someone,
we don't particularly like.

And sometimes

We do things together.

We plant a seed

We plant several seeds.

The block has a square of very dead grass.

No ball games

No loitering

No dogs

No fun

So

We dig it up.

                      We plant runner beans

Green beans

                      Tomatoes

Carrots

                      Potatoes

Enough to feed the whole estate

                      Fennel

Lettuce

                      Butternut squash

Chard

                      More chard

So much chard

            Like 'we might need to invent a collective noun
                  for chard' amounts of chard.

A really obscene amount of chard.

                      Chinese leaf.

<u>What</u> the Ant and Dec is that?

                      Chinese leaf.

That's not a Chinese leaf.

If anything it's a…

Somewhere-else leaf. It looks like it's wearing a burka.

            Okay. I don't think you can equate the pious
                  elegance of the burka with thick black rot

It is very dead.

                    Why is everything dead?

Something's growing.

                    Nothing's growing.

We'll try again.

        We can't try again. It's like a plague pit of vegetables.

It's not a /

An army of burka-wearing cabbages.

Sharia encroaches.

Okay. That's not funny.

It was a little funny.

You know that bit you've added about Muslims being the
fastest growing population on earth.

It's a fact.

I know it just sounds a bit scaremongery

It's true though.

I know it's true. It just sounds a bit racist.

I think you sound a bit racist.

What?

You're the one who thought it was scary.

I just said it as a fact.

You.

The racist.

Decided it was frightening.

I'm not a racist.

M'kay.

I'm not.

Sure.

How can I be a racist when…

What?

You what?

What because of me?

You think you can't be a racist because you're having
sex with me?

No I.

Donald Trump has slept with a lot of women.
Doesn't make him any less of a misogynist.

More of one if anything.

Yes.

So.

Actually. By that logic. Sexing me makes you more of a racist.

You are my white oppressor.

You are my glass ceiling.

You are /

Crying oh my god why are you crying?

I'm so sorry.

I was joking.

I thought we were.

I don't actually think you're a racist.

I think you're lovely. And great. And. Why are you crying?

Please tell me why you're crying?

I don't know.

You don't know?

I don't know.

Agh. Okay.

Um. Fuck.

I don't think I've ever actually seen you cry before.

I didn't really.

I didn't really think that was a thing that you did.

Can I /

No. You don't want me to touch you that's.
That's fine. I'm Sorry.

Please I beg you.

Please stop crying.

I'm sorry.

He gets on his hands and knees.

No I'm sorry.

I'm sorry I made you cry. And I. Please. Please stop /

Are you laughing or crying?

Bit of both.

Well that's half-good.

Do you really think I'm LovelyandGreat.

What? You've not. You've not really admitted that…
You've never.

Really, like said I'm a positive. Thing. In your life at all.

How stupid are you Daisy Taylor?

How could you not know that?

I quite like you on your knees.

Oh Yeah?

Yeah.

Okay. Do you like it when I do this?

Yeah. Yes.

Yeah, okay.

I mean if you wanted to, you know, make up for
the whole, 'calling me a racist' thing like, um…
Yep. Just kinda like. Yep. That's nice.

You've stopped crying.

Yep. Shut up. Keep going.

What?

What?

                        No nothing. You just. You just taste a bit different.
What!?

                                    Not like bad different.

Well obviously bad different or you wouldn't
have said anything.

            No not bad different. Just a bit, I dunno, just a bit sharper or,
                        I dunno discharge is a bit thicker /

                                    What are you doing?

What am I doing?

                            You're pulling up your knickers.

Yes of course I am. You just used the word discharge in a sexual
context which makes you essentially a psychopath.

                        I'm just saying your discharge /

I want to die.

                            Is a bit th-ick-er than normal.

            I think it's good if we feel comfortable talking about...
I feel sick.

                    I just wanted to check everything's okay with you.

Yes. Of course it is. Yes. It's probably just like an adjustment
period after I got my coil out.

                                            After.

You got your...

Coil out. Yeah. Since you got your vasectomy, I saw no reason to pump myself full of needless hormones, making myself fat and depressed.

Since I got my vasectomy.

Yes.

When did I get my vasectomy?

Um! I imagine the day after you waved your hospital letter at three hundred people shouting about getting a vasectomy 'tomorrow'!

You did get it didn't you?

Michael?

Yes! Of course, darling.

Of course, I did.

Ha. Oh my god.

Yeah I really got you right.

S'not funny.

So Daisy's pregnant.

No way dude. Congratulations.

Congratulations?

Yeah!

We're population activists with a combined salary of just under thirteen thousand pounds a year, and we live above a crackhead called Janice.

Oh. My. God.

What part of 'Daisy's pregnant' do you think sounds like a positive.

Um... The pregnancy test?

Right, strong joke that. Well worth sacrificing being there for me in my time of need.

<u>Michael's</u> best friend is a girl called Sarah which I used to be
really jealous about but now don't care at all because we're just
such great mates.

<u>So</u>, she gets an abortion, what's the big deal, OR leave her,
come out and be fun with me again. Stop spending nights in
watching *The Queen*.

                                                    The Crown.

The Crown. Which is shit B-T-Dubs.

                              Very high production values though.

How does that not make it worse?

What does Daisy think?

                    Oh she loves it, I think she secretly covets a tiara.

And about the pregnancy?

                                              Oh she doesn't know.

Right. You gonna tell her?

              I dunno, I'm guessing she'll probably figure it out.

Is it yours?

                                                         Yeah.

Would you rather, that it was yours, but you thought
that it wasn't.

OR

That it wasn't yours but you thought that it was.

                                    I'm not playing this game.

Would you rather have a nose made of bogey

Or a bogey made of nose.

                                                       Sarah.

Oh. Would you rather I died. Right. Not your fault. Of like,
polio or something.

Or, I survived, but you had tried to kill me and I knew that and
hated you.

                                                    First one.

Well that's fundamentally bad ethics.

You're gonna have to improve on that.

You know why, because You're Gonna Be A /

Dad.

Hi, um nice…. Er, nice, nice, curtains look I'm sorry that it's been a while.

Look I'm sorry that I stopped coming.

I never really meant to

I meant to, I never meant to make you feel unloved I brought you some flowers.

They're peonies, or pansies. They're not they're. Pegonias.

Begonias.

They're begonias. I. You need to plant them.

Me and Daisy we, we planted out window boxes for, our, neighbours and that

We're trying t' grow.

And we

I thought we could do it together.

Or not.

Or you and Daisy could

Daisy's here a lot. Isn't she.

Daisy loves you, Dolly I think you call her.

So that's good isn't it.

She's here [a lot] pregnant.

She's pregnant.

I suppose that's why I'm here

I think, I think I've been telling myself I haven't told her

Oh she doesn't know [by the way]

I think I've been telling myself I haven't told her because,
it's my fault and I

Oh it's [my fault] yep

Because it's my fault and I can't face, her, Cross, and

I think it's not that.

I think it's not that.

I think, what it is is, I, for the first time since, you looked at me
and didn't know know know know know

Didn't know who I was, did, couldn't,

For the first time I feel like

Connected?

Like literally the reason we're even together is

but, but I feel like maybe,

(We can't even raise a carrot)

I know, I think, somewhere you feel the absence of me,
I guess, and I'm really sorry about that. And it's not because
I don't love you

At all

It's basically the complete opposite of that.

It's because you are Everything I've Ever wanted to Be.

And the only person I've ever wanted to please.

And.

Just the thought.

Someone might look at me with half the /

That I look at you

Just

I would give ten years of my life

Or

Twenty.

Or.

But even that, wouldn't come close to enough.

There's just no [calculation] that /

I know we can't

But just for the minute

Just in this exact minute

I've got a family again

I've got a family again

And I'm not quite

Ready to let that go

He gasps.

Do you know what I mean?

Two. Ten.

Right

Time for *Countdown*!

Yep

Is it?

Is it?

Yeah. I'll get it going, I've got to

Go on

Janice put a fucking TV in the recycling bin today.

Not that

It makes a mockery of our recycling.

I know

Do you know what an effort it is to recycle?

Yes

And food. What is the point in sacrificing half our flat to
segregated recycling if she's gonna shit on it with her
Kentucky-fried telly

Jack?

I'm calling the council

How was Jack?

What I went to see him. It was fine.

Did he… [Recognise you]?

Did he, was he?

No, he didn't, he doesn't he never will
again, can we just watch whatever depressing
issue-based documentary

Kids on Xanax?

Mm

Plastic in the Ocean

Stop it you're making me hot

I feel like plastic in the ocean, is like, when you
need to piss and you sit down and the seat is
already like, soaked, and you are literally wet
with someone else's urine, but, by the time you
realise, it's so too late to do anything about it so
you just have to decide it's fine even though it's
totally not, and in your heart it makes you sick
but you have a false sense of calm in the face of
disaster. Know what I mean?

I don't sit down to piss so

Do you want turkey dinosaurs or sausages?

We should really go vegan

Yeah

Yeah

But one of us would need to learn how to cook.

Shotgun not   Shotgun not

Is that a gun?

Daisy

Daisy is it?

Don't confuse me.

I know you're Daisy.

Right. You know guns kill people, right,
you've not forgotten that one.

This one hasn't.

This was my father's.

He left Jamaica in 1943 with this gun and very little else.

For King and Country

It wasn't his country at the time but he certainly made it so.

Hard graft.

Laying down roots.

Would be a shame not to see that tree grow.

So he went off to war, didn't kill anyone, and
then he came home, here and he deactivated that gun,
so that future generations would never accidentally
shoot their sons' girlfr/latmate.

I have a favour to ask you Daisy.

I'm very happy, my boy found you

I feel I'm leaving him in good hands

Leaving. Booking a one way flight to
Switzerland are you?

I don't think there's any need to go that far.

Good. You scared me.

We can do it here.

Do what.

I need you to kill me Daisy. I'm not
strong enough to do it myself.

Oh good you've gone mental

I am mad Daisy I don't know my toes
from my toothbrush on a good day

And this is a bad day, is it?

>This is a great day. I know who I am. I know who you are
>and I know I want to die.

As a benchmark for a great day that seems pretty low

>Exactly.

>I've got maybe another forty like this.

>More maybe. Even.

>Life shouldn't be wasted on me

There are new souls who will make much more of it than me.

>Forty years of intensive medical care and
>a high-meat-content diet.

>That might come close to enough.

What are you talking about

>Kill me

No

>I want you to

>I'm running out of things I can do right

>Please

No.

>It's true, babies born in Britain add on average one hundred
>and sixty times more greenhouse emissions than babies
>born in Ethiopia

Hideous

>I think we should put it in the talk

Right

So like, hypothetically, if we were going to have a baby /

>Hypothetically.

Yeah

>Yeah?

We should have it in Ethiopia

                                        Yeah

Okay.

                                        Although

Quite a high infant-mortality rate

                                    Plus the air miles

Hardly worth it

                        Hypothetically hardly worth it.

Yep

Filthy, ungrateful short-sighted children rape their mother

Dig their nails into her flesh and squeeze oil from her breasts

Hungry

Greedy

They set fire to her hair and watch her tears run cold oceans

She spits back at them plague and drought but they laugh at her

They are clev'rer than her, she did not go to school

They have children of their own who now need to be fed

And while she clings on to life they can't fathom her dead.

Close your eyes close your ears and I'll end my harangue.

Cos our species been damned since that first great / [big bang].

                            What you thinking?

Meringue

                            I like meringue

Do you?

                                        Yeah

That is not a thing that I knew about you

                        Do you hate meringue?

No, but I was just thinking, I'd really love to make
a meringue right now but I bet Michael hates them.

> I don't hate them

Shall I make some meringue?

> Make some /

I brought you some mering/

Still got the gun then?

I swear to god if you accidentally shoot yourself
I Will kill you.

> Dolly?
>
> Oh Dolly I thought you were dead

Oh

> I had a horrible dream
>
> I've got to call to call to call my mum
>
> I told her that you died Dolly
>
> I told her you were dead

She's

Jack she's dead

She is dead

I'm not her and your mother's dead too

> She's
>
> How.
>
> She's
>
> Did I forget?

You forgot

> How could I forget?

I don't know

> Have I forgotten before?

Yes

I don't want to forget again.

Have a meringue.

I don't know if I like meringue.

Why don't you try?

I don't think I want to.

Okay

Is that okay?

That's okay

I had a steak and kidney pie for lunch.

Right.

It's a better taste to keep in my mouth.

No problem.

Give me your hands Dolly.

I'm not
She's dead

Almost.

Almost dead.

Saddest thing about me dying.

There's a lot of…

It's no proper home for you, in my addled brain Dolly.

I'm sorry I'm taking you out with me.

Jack I'm scared.

Don't be scared Dolly

We're going somewhere hotter.

He picks up the gun from his jacket and points it at her.

Give me your hands.

She slowly holds them up.

Give Me your hands.

She does. Slowly.

One here

He holds it to her stomach.

And one here

He holds her hand around the gun.

Tell him I love him.

Tell him you love him too.

And tell her about me.

Enough.

Bang.

<u>He</u> said it might be enough?

Yeh. Look I feel like you should be crying or something.
I dunno. I don't want to tell you how to feel but I did bring
home king-sized Kleenex.

Right did you buy those before or after you shot my father.

Hm!?

I didn't actually buy them. He had them in the house.
I used them to wipe my prints off the gun, and then
I thought, they might...

You thought you'd bring me Jack's wank
tissues as a memento.

Please don't. It's been a hard day.

Okay of all the people who should be telling other
people how to behave right now I think maybe
the one of us who's just shot the other's only
surviving parent is quite low on the general
hierarchy of... behaviour... issuing... people

He knew by the way

Knew what?

I mean, I know

Also

Probably something worth mentioning.

But I'm guessing that you told him.

> I don't know what you're talking about.

He said it might be enough

> He said it might be enough?

Yeh I.

> He said it might be enough.

Yep

> He heard me?

Okay

> He heard me!
>
> He heard me and then he fucking died

He starts to cry. She offers him a tissue which he takes.

> Do you think it was enough?

> So you don't think, it was enough?

Michael

> You're saying he just died, just, sacrificed everything for nothing.

No

> Well.

It'll still, do… good

> Oh well let's all just go and kill ourselves then, shall we.

I just.

The sums don't, the, of it, it doesn't

> No okay okay okay. Let's work this out.

What?

Let's work this out.

Okay

So, okay. What's the average life expectancy in the UK?

Seventy-nine point two years for males eighty-two
point nine years for females.

Okay, and this generation are expected to live

Twelve point two years longer.

Okay so that's ninety-one point four for men
and And ninety-five point one years for girls.

Women.

Ninety-five point one years?

For women yes.

Is that right?

That is the correct life expectancy for *women* yes. Why?

That's three billion seconds.

Huh.

Ninety-five point one years is three billion seconds.

How old was Jack?

Sixty next year.

Young.

Okay he'd've, so seventy-nine point two minus fifty-nine

Seventy-nine point two minus fifty-nine

Twenty point two

Okay so ninety-five point one minus twenty point two

You think it's a girl?

Seventy-four point nine

You think it's a girl.

Couple of billion seconds short

I think it's a girl

                    How many Jacks is that?

Three and three quarters

           Music starts up in downstairs flat.

                    How many Janices is that?

Fewer.

                  We can't actually kill Janice though

No

                              No

No

                              No

I mean

                              No

Right no.

                    Unless she wanted to

I mean I would want to if I was Janice

                  But you're not and she doesn't.

Shame.

                We should definitely go vegan though.

Yeah

                  I wish we had a car we could sell

We could buy a car, and then pretend to find out, and then sell it

                I don't think that's really in the spirit of

No

                Seventy-four point nine years to raise.

Seems like a lot.

                  We gonna have a baby?

Looks like it.

We're gonna have a baby.

Your dad's dead

My dad's dead.

Funny old day.

Yeah

I love you

I love you too

That's lucky because we're having a baby.

We're like grown-ups or something.

Wanna come to bed?

No I'm gonna go for a walk.

Don't get murdered

K

You're gonna be a daddy.

You're gonna be a daddy.

No I'm gonna be a mummy.

Fuck... yeah.

He goes for hours.

I think he would tell me what he was feeling if he knew

But he doesn't so [he walks]

I think I'd tell him what I was thinking. If I knew

But I don't so I eat cold turkey twizzlers out the fridge and remember I'm meant to be vegan.

I cover them in bleach.

Mrs Salinger I'm sorry you caught me reading the pap/

Daisy?

Were you reading the *Daily Mail*?

You don't have an appointment.

But you're a doctor.

Daisy, I'm sorry, I've told you if you are seeking an abortion you'll have to find another doctor to refer you.

No I know, I

I abstain on ethical grounds

Okay

I understand that teenage pregnancies are often unplanned.

People raise children in all sorts of circumstances Miss Taylor.

Right, I'm actually twenty-nine

Born in 1990 no?

Yeah

And you, ten in 2000, and oh, I appear to have lost a decade.

Right

Do you do that?

No

Extraordinary

Twenty-nine, really

I'd had five by your age

FIVE.

Declining birth rate in this country of course.

You youths today, you're very much younger aren't you?

In yourselves

Are we?

Yes

Why do you think that is?

Er… housing market?

Oh really

Well I'm afraid my ethical position doesn't change according to your age.

Right. S'not really very ethical though is it?

Well it's a matter of opinion.

Apparently.

I consider life to be sacred

I consider life to be sacred. I want to protect life on /

Then we're in agreement, Miss Taylor.

For You formed my inward parts; knitted me
together in my mother's womb.

I didn't.

God did.

Ah right. The *royal* You.

When I was being made in secret, intricately woven
in the depths of the earth. Your eyes saw my
unformed substance; in Your book were written,
every one of them, the days that were formed for me,
when as yet there was none of them.

I don't see it as man's business to burn God's books
before they've ever been read.

Nor do I as it happens.

I think it's a woman's business.

Very clever.

I am very clever. You're very stupid.

You may think what you like about me.

I interrogate my own beliefs very hard, Very regularly.

I have made my peace with God.

If you make the decision to terminate the pregnancy that
is your decision.

But I will play no part in it.

Well I'm keeping it, so.

That's wonderful news.

You didn't change my mind

> Of course. I'm delighted you have come
> to this commendable decision.

It's not Commendable though is it. It's actually madness.
It's actually a really stupid terrible selfish idea actually
and I have no idea how this has happened.

> I'm sure you have some idea.

> How it happened.

SLAM SLAM SLAM all through the night.
What time was it last night, what time did you
come home. And rattle my bones.

> Janice you smoke actual crack. You are
> a parody of a bad neighbour.

I don't smoke crack

> Okay

I

What? I don't

> No sure.

I really don't smoke crack.

> Good

I spent my morning at B&Q

> Great

I bought a Wandering Jew

> Okay, I don't know what that is.

It's a plant

> Lovely

I take care of it.

> Good for you

I'm a good neighbour

> Sure

I water your window boxes

> They're weeds. Dead weeds. You're watering Dead weeds.

I'm very quiet with the doors

> Good for you

Would you like me to teach you how to close the door?

> Not in the slightest. Look I'm only here because me and Daisy
> are getting rid of some meat

What's wrong with it?

> We're going vegan

What's wrong with you?

> Nothing, do you want it or not?

She takes one and sucks it.

Tastes like chemicals

> Well yeah, they're twizzlers.

I feel quite sick.

> Yes that's pretty common.

No I feel quite sick that I am joining your gang of mentalists
who shit out five babies and think people who have abortions
are sinners when actually they are our only hope. Abortionists.
Genetic… modifying scientists. Euthanasia-rists. They're the
heroes in this world. Not you sitting on your high Jesus horse
and telling them all they're going to hell.

> I'm actually very pro-GM food.

> Unlike my friends at the *Daily Mail* here.

> Still. A good firelighter though.

I don't have a fireplace

> Fuel. For. The. Fire.

> I agree.

> Look at this nonsense. Mice with six ears.

He gives her the paper.

All the more to feed ourselves with I say.

Ha ha.

But, on the sanctity of life the Bible is very clear.

We are created in God's own image and our lives
are to be respected.

No abortion. No euthanasia.

But you're keeping the baby Daisy, don't let it pray
on your mind.

I'm a euthanasiaRist though. I am. I am. I am.

Actually.

Fuck.

Yeah. I killed someone.

So roll that up in your Bible and smoke it.

Daisy you don't know what you're saying.

I do, no injections for me, I just shot him. Boom. Bang.

Daisy.

Miss.

Who did you shoot?

Michael's

Dad

'DaD'

Feels a funny word in my mouth.

Dad. Is. Dead

Daisy tells me my 'dad' has died

The police inform me that my 'dad' has died

The police but you have that patient–doctor confidentiality
thing. You can't. No but you actually can't. You can't tell
anyone anything that I said during a.

I go to the registry office and inform
them that my 'dad' has died

<u>No</u>, I didn't murder. I quite specifically.

> <u>I</u> am recommended a grief counsellor
> because my 'dad' has died

<u>I'm</u> not putting myself or anyone else in present danger

> <u>I</u> tell the woman in the corner shop who comments
> on the fact I don't usually buy cigarettes that
> my 'dad' had died

<u>I</u> leave you with very little option?

> <u>I</u> tell my friends that my 'dad' has died

<u>My</u> hands are hot and sweaty

> <u>They</u> give me sympathy because my 'dad' has died

<u>Please</u>

> <u>We</u> sit in long protracted silences because my 'dad' has died

<u>The</u> newspaper in my hands is shaking like it has a battery.

> '<u>my</u> dad' takes on a characteristic of his own

<u>Put</u> the phone down

> '<u>my</u> dad' weds me to everyone else whose 'dad' has died

<u>Stop</u> calling.

> '<u>my</u> dad' was not a person so much as 'my dad's dead'
> is a state of mind

<u>Please</u>

> <u>A</u> collective

<u>Please</u>

> <u>A</u> race

<u>He</u> wanted

> <u>A</u> new world religion praying to the god of my dad's dead

<u>Put</u> the phone down

> <u>And</u> I just want Jack to come and tell everyone
> they're stupid.

<u>Put</u> the phone down!

<u>I</u> turn on *Countdown*

One

    <u>Daisy</u> has left me tops and bottoms to three custard creams

Two

<u>She</u> only likes the middles

Three

'<u>And</u> I only like the biscuit bit.'

Four

<u>Is</u> what I said to her two years ago

Five

<u>Because</u> I wanted to have sex with her.

Six

<u>And</u> now she leaves me biscuits…

Seven

<u>Covered</u> in spittle

Eight

<u>All</u> over the house.

Nine

<u>God</u> this is a tedious programme

Ten

<u>Two</u> from the top.

Eleven

<u>Four</u> from the bottom.

Twelve

<u>Seventy-five</u>,

Thirteen

<u>One hundred</u>,

Fourteen

<u>Two.</u>

Fifteen

<u>Seven,</u>

Sixteen

<u>Four</u>

Seventeen

<u>and</u> nine

Eighteen

<u>Target</u>

Nineteen

<u>Nine hundred and forty-two</u>

Twenty

<u>One hundred</u>

Twenty-one

<u>plus seven</u>

Twenty-two

<u>One hundred and seven</u>

Twenty-three sheets of newspaper

<u>and</u> the two and the four

Three inches apart.

<u>So</u>, one hundred and thirteen

He watches me rolling them.

<u>Times</u> the nine

He's still on hold, God bless austerity.

<u>One thousand and seventeen</u>

Fold in half

<u>Take</u> the seventy-five

The pointed corners formed by each of the folds are
surprisingly sharp.

Nine hundred and forty-two

A grinning horde of Jihadis wielding EU passports
are daring me from the spine of my weapon. And:

Simple

How long. How long have you got left?

What?

They don't tell you I'm just.

On hold.

I'm sure they'll pick up soon.

How long have you got left. In your life?

How many years are you going to live?

Only He knows that.

Well, Can you ask him?

No.

Care to, take a guess?

I...?

You're a doctor aren't you?

Umm... twenty-something. Years.

Can you be more specific?

Er, twenty... twenty.

Twenty, twenty...?

Twenty-two years?

Twenty-two years.

Yes.

Hello! Police please.

Smack

Oh.

For the second time this week I go from being two of three
people in a room, to two of two, and it's like the whole universe
exists only within my body.

Nine times one hundred

My hands are covered in blood.

Two plus four is six.

She licks her hands.

Times seven. Right that is easier.

Tastes of rust and overstewed tea

Sometimes I overcomplicate life.

Twenty-two years.

She makes a note.

Jack would have said my way was more elegant.

Banked.

I'm hungry

There's nothing in the fridge

Oh the meat

Oh yes sorry I covered it all in bleach

You

I covered it in bleach. God you didn't eat it did you?

No, I um… threw it out

Phew

                                        Yeah phew

You seen Janice today?

                                        Er, no

She's throwing up more than I am.

                                        Is she?

Probably some bad spice or something

                                        Yeah, probably.

                                        How was the doctor's?

Oh fine, you know, wanted to know when my last period was
which was embarrassing because I couldn't answer.

                                        Right

I told him I was vegan

                                        Good

Felt funny saying it out loud you know.

                        We should watch your iron levels

Right yeah, he helped with that actually

                                        Supplements?

Yeah. Yep. Sort of.

                                        Cool

Blood-murder-blood-murder-blood-murder-blood-murder-
murder-murder-blood-POLICE!

Put your hand up, where I can see them, do put your hand up If
you are twenty-five or over

                                        You are old

Relatively speaking

                        If you're over twenty-five

You are older Than. The majority. Of the world's population

Genuinely

You are older than half the world

And you're only getting older

There are one point two billion people

Between the ages of ten and nineteen

That's a hell of a lot of teenagers

Now you might be thinking that's all smelly socks
and used condoms at bus shelters

But eighty-seven per cent live in the developing world

And as this new generation of prospective parents

Enter the sexual marketplace

Very few of them will have access to the
contraceptive services they deserve

This is the greatest issue facing mankind

This is where our energy needs to be focused

<u>This</u> is gonna start looking hypocritical

You're gonna start looking hypocritical

Well yes that's exactly my point

Look at your beautiful glowing hypocritical face

I'm not glowing

You're glowing

I'm sicky sweaty gleaming

You're beautiful sicky sweating gleaming

You're beautiful gaunt grieving

I'm okay

I hope you're okay

I'm okay

I'd already said goodbye in lots of ways

You knew whoever he was at the end better than I did

                                        Maybe that's what's hard
                                        I hope you're okay

I'm okay

                                        Okay

The police came round today

                                        What?

Yeah I know I shat myself

                                        Post mortem came back
                                        suicide

Well I know but I still

                                        What did they want?

Not for us, downstairs

                                        Oh

I know.

                                        And

Well they took something out in a body bag

                                        Did they?

Yeah

                                        Right

Poor Janice

                                        Yeah
                                        Did they
                                        The police
                                        Did they ask any questions?

No
I don't think
It's not suspicious is it
Local crackhead dies

Not gonna hit the news is it

She was clean

Yeah sure.

She was. She, bought a Wandering Jew.

Well, it only takes once. Doesn't it. Apparently,
you're more likely to die on a relapse than
anything else. Unless you can think /

Nah probably the relapse. Like. Amy Winehouse

Like Amy Winehouse, plus they cut it with all sorts like

Bleach?

Yes Sarah, bleach. I'm asking you, can you just google:
How much bleach would I have to drink to kill myself

Why can't you google it

I don't [wannit on]

My phone is loading really slowly and

Are you out of data?

Er, yeah

Are you okay for money?

Yeah

I mean no but

No more no than normal

I heard your dad died.

My dad died

Yeah, you didn't tell me about that.

Okay, sorry

I don't want you to be sorry I /

Good because I'm not

I wanna be there for you

> Great, so can you google, how much bleach,
> does it take to kill a person

I'm really worried about you

> I don't want you to be worried about me,
> I want you to pick up your phone and

Daisy said it was suicide

> When have you seen Daisy?

I didn't she, she put it on Twitter

> She put it on Twitter?

Yeah

> Well why did she put it on Twitter

It was national suicide prevention day

> So

So, so, she shared something and I was, It was
a bit of a weird tweet actually

> Daisy's weird on Twitter.

It had a Nike gif.

> Right.

And a Just Do It hashtag.

> You're worried about Daisy?

I'm worried about you.

> You don't need to worry about me

You just asked me to google how much bleach it
takes to kill someone,

Now either I'm worried about you,

Or I'm really worried about what you're gonna do
to someone else.

> Oh
> Right
> Yeah

Um

I think the baby it's

It's just been quite

Harder

I can't go any harder

You fucking can

Harder

I'm scared

Harder you fucking pussy.

I can't

You can

I'm scared I'm gonna hurt it

You're scared you're gonna hurt It?

Sorry

You're?

It's a mouse Michael

I know

You're, you're, meant to hurt it, you're trying to kill it

I know

The aim of hitting it with a bat, is surely, to frickin kill it

I want to kill it, I just, I don't want to hurt it, I don't
wanna like half-kill /

Give me the bat

No

Give me the bat Michael

No, you'll hurt the baby

Then kill the effing mouse

I'm just

They carry diseases which could kill your baby.

> Feeling a bit overwhelmed at the moment and I was
> wondering if we could let this one live.

Oh

Sorry

Don't be sorry

I feel like an idiot

Don't

I just

I just wanna bath

Okay

Okay

Do you wanna bath together?

Okay

Okay

I bought a new candle from Aldi

It's a Jo Malone rip-off

Peony blush

It smells

Good

Good

It's in my bag

Where's your bag?

In our room

I'll get it

He leaves.

You are very cute. But I'm still gonna

Murder

Meat is murder.

But its not cows we're talking about.

Meat.

Is murdering you. Your brothers and sisters.

Us.

People.

All human kind.

Our planet is finite.

Our resources are finite.

Our arable land is

Infinite.

No only joking it's finite.

Earth has one point billion hectors of arable land.

That is enough to sustain a maximum of ten billion people.

If.

And only if.

We all /

ALL

Go vegetarian.

Even you porker.

You're getting fat

I know

It's lovely

It's very lovely.

I went to Janice's funeral today.

How was it?

Sad.

Yeah?

Well no, not really.

I find myself checking the news constantly

Praying for tsunamis

Earthquakes

Droughts

Ebola

Dear God bring back Ebola

Please

Bring back HIV

Bring back Stalin

Don't ban the bomb

Bomb the shit out of somewhere, everywhere I'm not

And please, please some make space for my
beautiful, beautiful baby girl

I want her to inherit the Earth and if she's going to do that then
you can't have it too

Dal?

What's that now?

Lentils

Looks like death

Does yeah, which is ironic really, given how
much of the food we used to eat was actually dead.

I more meant it looks like it would kill me.

No one ever died from lentil.

I'm sure it will be delicious.

I'm sure it won't be. (Careful it's hot.)

You cooked for me

I cooked for you

                                        Look at us

I know

Knock at the door.

Can you get that?

                              It'll just be Bible-bashers.

Well get rid of them quickly.

                                             Okay

They kiss. He leaves.

I can't wait lentil…

Some pun or other that I'm glad you've walked out of the room
and can't hear me fail to make.

                                                Hi

Hi

                               You better come in.

I love you lentil the end of the. No. I Lent-tilly, no I'll wait for
Len-til

                                          Daisy.

Oh you made me jump.

                        Can you explain this to me.

Oh, I was just trying to make a lentil pun to, I didn't get,
anywhere

Oh.

Janice. Hi.

                 Janice bought us some oil for our door hinges.

And some slippers for you love.

                       To say thank you apparently.

Nice and cosy. No need to wear hard-soled shoes
on that hard wood floor of yours. Take it right out
of your toes.

That's very kind Janice.

Very kind Janice.

Surprising too.

Not that surprising Janice has always been very kind.

You alright love you look like you've seen a ghost.

Do I?

Are you a ghost Janice? That could feasibly
make sense of this situation.

Am I a. Ghost? What are you [talking about]?

No just Michael's sense of humour. Ha ha ha.

Oh ha ha ha. I don't get the joke

Don't listen to him he's mad I think he's probably actually
clinically insane.

He a drinker love?

Vegan, twice the rates of mental instability.

Is that right? Although I don't recommend eating that
meat he was on. I brought it straight back didn't I Dais.
What was it I said.

…Can't remember.

Tastes like it's been covered in bleach. Best in the bin. We did
have a laugh didn't we Dais.

Did you. Ha. Ha. Ha. That is funny.

Anyway, I've only come round to say thank you
for those train tickets, imagine you having spares to [place]!
And that where my sister and her girls are. I don't see
them enough you know. I feel ten years younger.
Eric's talking now.

It wasn't a problem.

It meant a lot to me.

We had a cancelled tour date there so.

>   No we didn't

Yes we did.

>   Mm… Don't think we did.

We did that's why I had tickets to give Janice.

What's up with him.

>   Sorry,

>   Janice,

The 'trip' I was led to believe that we possibly accidently 'gave
you tickets for'

>   I just was led to believe was a little more.

>   Unfortunately.

>   Long-term.

>   And um…

>   I'm just slightly…

>   um… confused,

>   Really,

Because Daisy was actually the one who told me, about your

>   Long-term travel plans.

>   and yet she seems somewhat less surprised
>   than me that you're, back.

>   So, soon.

Michael. Sweetheart can I talk to you in the
boiler cupboard a minute.

Very close.

Ah… yeah. So. Funny story.

Okay so I'm getting the impression Daisy that you not only led
me to believe that Janice was dead, but also that you
deliberately engineered it so that I might think that I killed her.

                                        Tell me I'm crazy.
                                Daisy tell me I'm crazy.

I just wanted you to feel involved.

                                            Involved!?

Shhh. I just. I wanted you to feel like you were providing. I
wanted you to feel. I wanted you to feel like a man. Like a dad.

                                    By killing Janice?!

I've got something to show you.

    Ooh what could it be, your decapitated parents under the bed?

Ha ha. Very funny. My parents are not coming into this house.

Dead or not dead.

Okay.

I need you to not freak out.

        Well that might be easier, sweetie, if you hadn't just tried to
                                        frame me for murder.

Don't call me sweetie, it just feels patriarchal and I hate it.

Like, even in anger, particularly in anger.

And I didn't; try and frame you for murder.

I only wanted You to think that.

I didn't want, you know, anyone else to think that.

                                        Right. Okay.

Okay.

Okay.

So, this is a really good thing okay. Ready.

Okay.

Here.

It's a spreadsheet

It's a spreadsheet.
With a pie chart.

With several pie charts

For our daughter.

Okay

So here is ninety-five point one years. Three billion seconds

I see that

It's the
Whole pie
The target

Right

This piece of pie
Is twenty-point two. That's.
Jack.

Oh
Oh. Oh.
Oh.
Daisy.

This piece of pie

The massive one

No the little one, three point seven this piece of
pie is us going vegan.

I can't see it

It's very small

What's the big piece of pie?

This piece of pie is just other bits and pieces I've been doing.

                                        Like what

I made my own deodorant

                          It's a massive piece of pie

And I

                                            Yeah

Am using bar shampoo

          It's a massive twenty-two-year piece of pie Daisy

I killed that mouse

                          Those live for like what, a day?

And maybe also my doctor

                                           What?

Hm?

                                             You

                                       You killed

My doctor yes.

                                             You

                                             You

He wasn't very nice. Also he's an anti-abortionist in
a position of medical power so the net gain is probably
even better exponentially better... but... but I thought
I'd keep it simple.

                                            You.

                                            How?

With a newspaper.

                                           When

Does it matter?

                                   No just curious!

You're raising your voice, and that's bad for the baby

Oh right and how was bludgeoning a general
medical practitioner? For the baby?

You're gonna go to jail.

I doubt it. Mrs Salinger's already been accused.

Who's Mrs Salinger? Why's she been accused?

Because I took her appointment.

Well she's not gonna confess

No, well no.

She hung herself, couldn't face the questioning.

I thought about putting that on the spreadsheet but
I thought it would be a bit scavenger

Scavenger

Scavenger-ish

Okay.

Okay.

This is a lot.

I know, I /

Something is knocked off the side. They both freeze.

I'm just a. Little bit tired. I'm gonna leave the slippers.
You enjoy those.

Night.

We've got to kill her.

She didn't hear.

Did she hear?

No.

You go outside. And I'll say something. And you tell me if you
can hear me.

Okay

He leaves the cupboard.

So at this volume did Janice hear about all the murdering?

No.

She leaves the cupboard.

Okay so that's a yes we've got to kill her.

What?

> Daisy I've had five minutes of not having thought
> I killed Janice and I have to say I enjoyed them.

Look at her. Look at her. She's guzzling oil and water
and farting carbon. She's death. She's fucking everything
up and she isn't even grateful.

Daisy.

She's stupid. She's gonna have loads more kids that are all
gonna be put in care too and then have loads of kids
themselves because no one's gonna teach them about condoms.

My kids aren't in care.

Don't listen to her, she's lying, you see them what once every
six months for a couple of weeks and they're gone again.

They're my grandkids. I'm fifty-six.

She's gonna eat pizzas plugged into a ventilator till she's ninety
watching *Britain's Got Talent* wearing sweatshop Primark.
She's gonna buy crack smuggled in up the arseholes of South
American children.

I have never and would never smoke crack.

She's gonna buy eight metres of wrapping paper every
Christmas and birthday.

I.

She's gonna buy a bag for life every time she goes shopping
and throw them all away.

She'll buy three-for-two Easter eggs and put the packets in landfill.

She'll buy a diesel car and drive it to the shops and back.

She'll drop fag butts on the floor.

I quit smoking.

She'll put a fucking straw in every Archers and lemonade she orders till the end of time.

She'll have fish-and-chip Fridays and she won't even think about the plastic in the ocean Despite having seen *Blue Planet*.

She'll take home shit shampoo and conditioner bottles to remind her of all the shit places she's been.

She'll leave the radio on when she's out so burglars will think someone's home.

She'll buy books she'll never read.

I've got a library card.

She'll buy Fruit Shoots for her grandkids and treat herself to a Diet Coke.

She'll buy plush toilet paper that's not even recycled.

She'll buy Flash Wipes.

She'll use Tampax, and I bet she has a heavy flow.

I'm fifty-six?

She'll make the fatberg worse.

She'll eat ten cows and twenty-seven chickens a YEAR for loads more years.

She'll eat irresponsibly sourced palm oil.

She'll burn down the rainforest.

She'll put plastic bags in the food-waste bin.

She'll own three more tellies and put them all in the recycling.

SLOP. CRASH. BANG.

Oh my god.

Oh my god.

You've got dal everywhere.

Janice?

And you've chipped the Le Creuset. Jesus.

Janice.

Is she.

You told me to.

I told you to kill her. Not.

Is she dead?

Uh. No.

She's breathing.

She is knocked out though. And pretty burnt. Should be pretty easy now.

You could probably get her to choke on the lentil.

Just hold her head in it.

No

Be really easy.

I can't

For the piece of pie.

Let's work it out.

What out, who who are you calling?

The piece of pie; life-expectancy calculator.

Janice is. Fifty-six. Female. White. Education – what do you think? Secondary? Divorced. Not currently working.
Income under, never exercises. What would you say five-four?
A hundred and twenty pounds? General health – poor.
Diabetes Janice? No. Drinks. Eight or more. Smoking.

She said she quit.

Let's go smoker.

Calculate.

Ah I've gotta put in a email address.

Oop. Hang on.

What's my password?

No.

Yep.

Seventy-six.

                                        Twenty years.

Twenty years.

                        I can't. I can't. Get how you do this.

                        I know I thought. I know I. Maybe said.

                                                    But.

                        It's Janice. Bleeding. In our kitchen.

                                            I can't bear it.

                        She might die. She might die die.

                        And if I kill her then I'm a murderer.

                                                 Forever.

                And when it was the bleach it was. But now it's.

                                                    An.

                                                 I just.

He hits himself in the head.

She stops and calms him.

hey, hey, hey. You can murder a hundred times as many people
with a vote. Or not even vote a purchase. Buy a gram of coke,
fuck it a can of Coke. How many people have died getting that
to [you] / this is responsible. This isn't some head in the sand
won't get your hands dirty starve the foreign kids. This is us
properly accounting for our child. This is us, increasing the net
happiness of the world. This is

This is Janice.

This is Janice.

How can you...?

How can you.

I don't know what I'm asking you.

How can you look at her?

It's not me. It is me. It's having this, her in me. It's like she's
woken something up in me. From like the oldest parts of me.
Like the very first bit of. From like the animal. Soul of me.
And like I've finally understood what I'm meant for.
Found something that I can do. Something that I can grow.
Something that is mine and perfect and I would kill anything
to protect. And I love you. And I care about this family.
It's just. Weeding. If we wanna do this right we've got
forty-nine point two years left to raise. And I would sacrifice
anyone Everyone for that. 'Cept me. And You. And Her.

I just want you to be in this with me.

Daisy.

I can't believe that you can't.

Are you in this with me?

Give me the pan.

MICHAEL *gives* DAISY *the lentil pan which she
uses to drown Janice.*

Twenty-nine point two to go.

> MICHAEL *cries, he can't look at Janice's body.*

<u>You</u> alright?

> I've never seen your body before

Shut up you're making me self-conscious

> I sort of didn't really figure you had one

Like a floating head

> No so, clothes, stuffed with like
>
> Like a scarecrow

Like a scarecrow?

> Yeah
>
> A SaaarahCrow

Okay

> It's nice to see you.

I don't know why we didn't go to the ladies' pond it is
SO much nicer

> Do you not?

You could have dressed up or something.

> Could I?

The sacrifices I make for you.

> What?

The water is fucking murky here

> Can we get in I'm getting cold

That makes. Literally no sense.

> GO

Let me finish my cigarette.

> I really hate that you smoke.

I really hate that you have made some recent life choices and
are trying to enforce them on all your friends.

Smoking kills.

Not that you have any friends any more.

They'll kill you

Nah.

They will.

I don't have a pension.

The NHS is collapsing.

I am not being an old person in this country.

I'm taking myself out in a blaze of glory the day
I turn sixty.

That's mad.

Unless, I accidentally do it before then
attempting an ill-advised DIY project.

You're thirty now.

Exactly. I'm only halfway through. And the first
half's taken ages.

If the next thirty, or well, twenty-nine-and-a-little-bit
years take half as long as the last I've got loads of time.

Right.

And I won't have to deal with all my teeth and
pubes falling out.

–

Do you reckon there's dead bodies at the bottom of the pond?

No

Dead fishies

Jump

Keep your Speedo on

I'm gonna push you

Don't

He does.

(*Splutter*.) Oh my god that was such a breach of trust.

I have actual water up my actual nose and I am going to actually kill you.

I'm sorry.

Well fucking get in then.

Yeah.

You can't push me in and then do your little swimwear parade up down the /

'It's lovely once you're in.'

Sorry.

I said it's lovely once you're /

He jumps in.

Oof Jesus.

Hello

Hey what are you doing

Can you not swim?

Michael, you should have

told

me

you can't

Swim

Michael, I can't hold you

I love you

You've got to let go you're

(you love me like you... l)

me under

Please

I can teach

Float

Oh my god Michael I thought you were going to

Drowning sounds.

Just.
Stop

Panicking.

Let

Let

Me get us to the buoy.

Fuck ow.

You. Punched me.

Michael I thought you were gonna
You're swimming!
You're doing it.

You're amazing.

Look at.

You could always swim.

You.

You weren't drowning.

                                                    Don't

Don't what.

You.

Were

you, trying

to kill me

                                        Don't realise that.

Why?

Why?

                                        Because now I have to.

                        Beat.

                        Gasp.

Michael

                        Drowning.

                                –

The following is very loving.

<u>Honey</u> you're home.

I'm In.

In.

Yeah, I Can.

You can?

I Did

You Did?

I did.

You did!

Ninety-five point one.

Ninety-five point one?

Three billion seconds.

Three billion seconds.

Done.

Done?

Done.

Do you wanna [talk]?

No

Telly?

Sex?

Telly and sex?

I could telly and sex

Takeaway?

Chinese?

Vietnamese?

Thai, compromise Thai

Chicken?

                                        Yes

Really.

                                        Beef

Beef?

                            You deserve beef.

You won't tell the spreadsheet

                    We've completed the spreadsheet

You look pretty

                            You look pretty

I want to have sex with you now

                                        Yeah?

Yeah?

                                        Yeah?

Yeah?

                                        Yeah

Yeah

                                        Yes

Yep

                                        Yeah

Yeah

                                        Yes

Yes

                                        Yes

Fuck

                            That was quick

Fuck

And more than

Mmmmm

Oh fuck

Yes

Fuck

Taxi

Dialling

Ooooohh

Breathe

Breathe

Breathe

Breathe

Breathe

Breathe

Breathe

Breathe

Breathe

Breathe

Breathe

Breathe

Breathe

Breathe

Breathe

Breathe

Breathe

Breathe

Breathe

Breathe

Breathe

Breathe

                                              Breathe
Breathe

                                               Breath
Pain

                                                 Face
Pain

                                          I love you
Pain

                                              Breathe
Pain

                                              Breathe
Pain

                                              Breathe
Pain

                                              Breathe
Pain

                                              Breathe
Pain

                                              Breathe
Pain

                                              Breathe
Pain

                                              Breathe
Pain

   Breathe

Pain

                                                       Breathe

Pain

                                                       Breathe

Pain

                                                       Push

Pain

                                                       Push

Pain

                                                       Push

Pain

                                                       Push

Pain

                                                       Push

Pain

                                                       Push

Push

                                                       Push

Push

                                                       Push

(*Gasp.*)

                                                       Crying

Crying

                                                       Sleep

Seven pounds

                                              Eleven ounces

Can't Sleep

                                    Crying
Tired

                                    Crying
Tired

                                    Laugh
Her

                                    Him
Another

                                    Them
Eight pounds four ounces.

                                    Bigger.
Six billion seconds

                                    Tired
So Tired

                                    Sleep
Crying

                                    Laughing
Mummy

                                    Daddy
Morning

                                    Morning
Mummy

                                    Daddy
Daughter

                                    Son
Catchment

Baby yoga

Fingers Out

Mummy

Daddy

Eat your peas

You can't only eat steak

He can

Meat

Muscle

Stronger

Bang

Oopsie daisy.

Fragile

Three foot four

Wall

Mark

Taller

Older

Bigger

Better

Bath

Bed

Hungry

You're too heavy for a carry

Just

No

No

No

                                                No

No.

                                             Okay.

No!

                                             But.

Okay.

                                             Just

Okay

                                             Just

Grow

                                            Grow

Grow

                                            Grow

Grow.

ALCATRAZ

Nathan Lucky Wood

NATHAN LUCKY WOOD

Nathan Lucky Wood grew up in London. He was a member of the Soho Theatre Writers' Lab. His previous play, *A Haunting*, premiered at the King's Head Theatre in 2016 before transferring to VAULT Festival and the Belgrade Theatre, Coventry. His work has been seen at the Bush Theatre, Arcola Theatre, Southwark Playhouse, Leicester Square Arts Theatre, Rich Mix, and Theatre503.

Alcatraz was first performed at VAULT Festival, London, on 27 February 2019, with the following creative team:

Director	Emily Collins
Producers	Ellie Fitz-Gerald and Emily Davis
Designer	Lizzy Leech
Lighting Designer	Rachel Sampley
Sound Designer	Annie May Fletcher

At the time of going to print the play was still to be cast.

Characters

SANDY, *a girl*
PETER, *a young man*
ARDEN, *his boss*
DONNA, *a granny*
VOICES *of* OBERSTURMBANNFÜHRER, ESTATE AGENT,
    PRIEST *and* OFFICER
CLINT EASTWOOD
DANIEL, *Sandy's dad*

CLINT EASTWOOD, DANIEL *and the* VOICES *to be played
by the same actor.*

Note on Text

If a line ends without punctuation, but the next line is the same
speaker, then it usually means they are struggling to find the
right words. If the next line is a different speaker, it means the
next line follows on quickly.

1

SANDY, *eleven years old, in her pyjamas, sturdy boots, and a rucksack over her shoulder. She is standing on a window ledge.*

SANDY. First, what you do is, you blow up a balloon. Then you tear up strips of paper and you put them in the paste. And then you put the pastey paper round the balloon until there's no balloon it's all just paper. And then it dries. And what you should have, is what looks like, a head.

If it doesn't look too much like a head now, that's okay. It's not shaped like a head, it's shaped like a balloon, 'cause that's what it is. But if you put a nose on it looks better. You just scrunch up pastey paper into a nose shape. And then you wait for it to dry –

And then when it's dry you get to paint it!

Now. This is important. Miss B will tell you, you can paint it any colours you like. She'll say, why not paint it rainbows. Why not paint stars on it. Why not paint a beautiful sky. She'll say, look at Omar's work. Omar's painted a field with a rabbit. Omar's painted a sun with a face. She'll start to cry a bit 'cause she loves the rabbit and the sunface so much. She'll say, why can't you do something like Omar? Why can't you try, for once, to make something nice? DO NOT LISTEN TO HER. A HEAD IS A HEAD IS A HEAD. It doesn't have stars or rainbows or rabbits. It's got wrinkles and liver spots and it ain't smiling 'cause no one smiles when they're sleeping. Miss B can say what she likes. She can write a report, say you lack imaginative capacity. The sun don't have a face or if it does we don't know, 'cause if you look at the sun you go blind.

And she's not seen the movie.

My favourite movie, and the best movie in the whole world, is – *Escape from Alcatraz*. It's a true movie. It's got my favourite actor Clint Eastwood. When I grow up I'm going to be Clint Eastwood. I know that's not currently possible but it didn't used to be possible to go to the moon or for girls to go to university, so. You know. Who cares what who says what is possible.

In the movie they're in Alcatraz which is the worst prison ever in the world. No one's ever escaped from Alcatraz. The walls are thicker than an entire house and outside the walls it's just water. You're locked in your cell every night, and every half-hour the screws come and check you're sleeping, so even if you did get out you wouldn't have time to get away, they'd know you were gone and they'd be after you and get you. When you're locked up in there you're locked up there till you die. Except Clint Eastwood, he digs through the wall WITH A SPOON and he makes a fake head to fool the screws and he gets away. So it used to not be possible to escape from Alcatraz, until it was.

Dad says I can have a key when I'm twelve. But it'll be too late then. So it's got to be the window.

It's cold. But not real cold. Not cold like rowing across San Francisco Bay on a raft made of stolen raincoats is cold. This is just breezy.

And then you jump.

She jumps.

Blackout.

2

ARDEN *is sat at a desk. She is holding a piece of tinsel.*

She is seven months pregnant.

PETER *is standing in front of her.*

ARDEN. Do you know what this is?

PETER. Um. It's tinsel.

ARDEN. That's right, Peter. Tinsel.

> *Beat.*

> What can you tell me about tinsel?

PETER. It's a Christmas decoration. It's for putting on things.

> To make them Christmassy.

ARDEN. Yes, that's right. That's it exactly. It's for putting on things. Things, Peter. Things.

> Have you been to Mrs Connolly's room today?

PETER. Not today

ARDEN. Well I have. And what I found is, she's taped black all over the windows, turned all the lights off, and she's sat there in her armchair, with this all wrapped round her head like she's a bloody Christmas tree.

> Is Mrs Connolly a thing, Peter?

PETER. No –

ARDEN. Where do you think she got this, Peter?

PETER. Er

ARDEN. 'Cause what Mrs Connolly said is, and this is a quote, 'the nice man gave it me'. So I've been sat here racking my brains a bit, trying to think, who could it be – someone who works here – who's *nice*.

> Peter? Can you think of anybody?

PETER. Oh – I don't –

ARDEN. *Nice*. We're looking for *nice*.

PETER. I think everyone's nice –

ARDEN. No, they're not, Peter, I'm afraid you're wrong about that. Everyone who works here is not *nice*. What we are, is *professional*. Which means when the residents come to us asking for us to give them a bit of tinsel to wrap around their heads, we think, is that a sensible, safe, *professional* care decision.

And we say *no*.

Did you give Mrs Connolly this?

PETER. Um. The thing is, she – she thinks we're doing something to her brain. It stops her sleeping and. The tinsel – she thinks the tinsel keeps the signals out –

ARDEN. Peter, I don't care what she thinks! She's a vulnerable old woman with symptoms of paranoia, and this is a serious choking hazard! We don't let her have it because we don't want her to die!

Peter, next year it won't be me sat in this chair. It'll be whoever head office sends in as my cover. And I promise you, they won't care how *nice* you are. If you get found doing anything like this, you'll just be gone. Like that. Do you understand that?

PETER. Yes.

ARDEN. Is it just Mrs Connolly?

PETER....No.

ARDEN. How many?

PETER. Um – quite a few on the fourth floor – she's been telling them about it and she's quite popular – they all wanted to try it –

ARDEN. Jesus, Peter!

Listen to me. They're doing inspections now. They come in secret. Like mystery shoppers. Could be anyone. A visiting family member. Even a new member of staff. Anyone new you see here could be one. For all we know there could be someone here right now!

What do you think would happen if an inspection happened and they saw this?

PETER. I'd be fired?

ARDEN. Yes! You'd be fired.

PETER. Please Miss Arden – I'm really sorry

ARDEN. Okay, god, don't cry or anything. Look, here's what I want you to do. Go round the whole home. Collect up all the tinsel, baubles, everything, all the decorations. Put them all in a big box. Bring them to me here so I can check you've got everything. And then take the box down to the incinerator. And burn it.

PETER. Burn it?

ARDEN. Burn it?

PETER. But – it's Christmas –

ARDEN. Well you should have thought of that before you started indulging them in this. There's no rule that says we have to have decorations up, Peter. There's definitely a lot of rules that say we should not allow the residents to choke to death on a festive bauble.

Okay?

PETER. Okay.

ARDEN. Piss off then.

Blackout.

3

SANDY. I thought the canal would be empty. During the day
it's all just people walking dogs, and no one does that at
night. But it's not. There's people. In the bushes. First I just
see a bit of blue in the bush. I go over to look. It's a sleeping
bag. And in the sleeping bag it's a man inside it. He looks
like he's older than my dad *twice*. He's got a big Santa beard,
'cept it's not white it's sort of grey and yellow and bits of it
are black, and you can tell it's not a fake one 'cause you can
see it go right into his face.

Further on there's more of 'em. Men in bags. Some of them
not even hiding, just right down on the path. It's all men
I think. Don't think I see any women.

Most of the way you've got canal on one side and bushes on
the other, with a wall behind 'em. But if you keep going the
wall gets smaller, and then it's just a fence, and then the
bushes open out a bit, and then you can see through the fence
and it's there.

Alcatraz.

It's huge. Like some old castle or something. Like you could
lock up my whole school inside, all the kids and all the
teachers, and still have room for more. All the men in the
bags I seen, they'd fit inside. You could put everyone I've
ever known, every person I've ever met in my life, inside,
and lock 'em up, and never see 'em again, I reckon.

The fence is old and rusty but still, it takes ages, even with
Dad's boltcutters. And there's someone watching. One of the
men's woken up and he's looking at me. He's lit a cigarette
and when he puffs it I can see his eyes. Puff. Red. Just
looking. I say HELLO WHAT ARE YOU LOOKING AT
PLEASE but he don't say nothing back. Just puff. Red eyes.
And then I give the boltcutters another push and I don't have
to say anything more 'cause I'm through.

There's a light on the second floor, otherwise it's dark. I go
round the ground till I find an open window. There's one. Get
in, crawl through, drop down, and this is it – I've made it –

I'm in a cell. It's small. Not like the ones in the movie but
still. There's barely nothing in it except a TV and a bed.

TV's on, just static. I go through all the channels to try but they're the same.

And in the bed there's the man. And he is so old. He's got old-people face, all wrinkly with brown spots on it. When he breathes he makes a funny sound like scrunching paper. His eyes are open and he's looking at me.

Hello?

He don't say nothing back. Just looks at me. Not surprised like. Just like I crawl in his window every day.

He's got a halo of tinsel, like an angel, all round his head.

Hello Mr Smelly Old Angel Man. Which way is it to Mrs Quexis' room please?

He don't say nothing. His eyes just slide off me back to the TV. Bye bye then Mr Angel.

The corridor's all doors with numbers. The one I been in is a hundred and twelve. And this is just one floor! I need a plan –

Lights snap on. We're in the corridor. PETER *has just entered, with armfuls of tinsel, and turned the light on, to see* SANDY.

PETER. Hey!

You shouldn't be in here! We're closed! How'd you get in? Who are you? Where's your parents?

SANDY. What are you doing with that?

PETER. With what?

She points at the tinsel. He tries to hide it.

Nothing.

SANDY. There's a man in there with that all wrapped round his head.

PETER. Where?

SANDY. A hundred and twelve. Are you doing that? Are you putting tinsel on people's heads?

PETER. I'm not

SANDY. Is it a Christmas thing? He don't seem very festive. Is he okay?

PETER. Who?

SANDY. The tinsel man.

PETER. Have you looked in all these rooms?

SANDY. Just that one. Why did you do that?

PETER. I didn't –

SANDY. It's like a Christmas hat, isn't it. That's nice. I think that's a nice idea. Next time though you should use a proper hat so it doesn't fall off. Tinsel's for trees, not people.

PETER. We don't have a tree.

SANDY. Don't have a tree? It's Christmas Eve.

PETER. We never got one.

SANDY. So you put it on people's heads? That makes sense. Only you should make sure no one goes to sleep in a tinsel hat, or what if when they breathed in they breathed in a bit of tinsel and choked and died

PETER. No one's going to die! I'm dealing with it.

How'd you get in here anyway? No one's supposed to be here. What are you doing?

SANDY. Just looking round. Inspecting.

PETER *looks at her in panic*.

PETER. Well I'm collecting all this and taking it down and disposing of it, right now, so don't worry!

SANDY. What?

PETER. Getting rid of it, all of it, it's all going in the furnace

SANDY. That's silly, it's Christmas, put it up.

PETER. What?

SANDY. Put it up. Put it up there.

PETER. I'm not supposed to –

SANDY. That's stupid.

PETER. Is it?

How old are you?

SANDY. Old enough. Why? What's it to you?

PETER. You seem a bit young to be a

SANDY. To be a what?

PETER. An inspector.

Beat.

SANDY. No. Not really. I think I'm the perfect age. They use kids for all the inspections now. People don't see you coming when you're this age. Don't think you can do anything clever. Let you ask all kinds of questions. You answered all my questions, didn't you? Didn't see me coming. I've found out a lot already. I know you lied about putting tinsel on the man. This inspection's going really well. Making lots of progress. Just got a few things to clear up and then you can be on your way. Okay?

PETER. Um

SANDY. Why'd you put the tinsel round their heads?

PETER. I didn't

SANDY. Yes you did. You did and now you're trying to get rid of it before someone finds out. You think I don't notice things? I do notice things. I notice a cover-up when it's in front of me. People underestimate you when you're a kid. That's why they use us for this kind of work. That's twice you've lied now and I'll remember.

He is on the verge of tears. SANDY *takes pity on him.*

It's alright. I forgive you.

She holds out her hand.

Inspector Eastwood. And you are?

PETER. Peter. I, um, I work here.

SANDY. And what are you going to do with all that, Peter?

PETER. Burn it.

SANDY. Wrong. You should put it up.

PETER. But I was told

SANDY. Well now I'm telling you different. What I'm telling you is, it's time for you to be a bit more imaginative. I'm going to be writing a report on this whole place. I'm going to be writing it on you. There'll be a whole page, just about Peter. What am I going to say on that page? Am I going to say, Peter doesn't know how to do a Christmas?

Look at this place. It's like a prison.

Put a bit there.

He does.

There. Doesn't that look nice?

Aren't you happy now we've put it there?

PETER. Um

SANDY. You know what your problem is, Peter? You lack imaginative capacity.

PETER. I know, they told me that in school.

SANDY. Well, don't worry. You don't really lack imaginative capacity, you just – don't know how to use it yet. I can train you. Listen to me, and you'll pass the inspection with a very good mark.

PETER. I'm being marked?

SANDY. Of course.

But I need your help first, Peter.

I need you to help me find someone.

4

DONNA *is sat upright, holding tinsel wrapped round her head.*

There is a faint background sound of white noise and static.

DONNA. It was a moonlit night. No… drenched. A moon-drenched night. Drenched? What are you on about, Donna? It was just night!

The sound of the static increases. Perhaps we can hear fragments of voices in it. DONNA *adjusts the tinsel on her head and it subsides.*

Night. And even the stars were dark. That's good. We came in as low as we could, on a plane with its wings painted black. The only light was the town behind the hills, its searchlights up to the sky, and its guns –

The static has been building up again. Suddenly there is a voice from out of it:

OBERSTURMBANNFÜHRER. And so ve haff you at last, Mrs Quexis! The Vixen herself, at the mercy of the Thousand-Year Reich –

She moves the tinsel quickly and the voice fades away. Another voice:

ESTATE AGENT. It's a steal, love, a steal, take a tip from me. All modern, insulated, all mod cons –

DONNA. Oh, shut up!

ESTATE AGENT. Shut up? I wish I could, I only wish I could! But I'm too moved, moved by the beauty of this estate. It's the first wave of the future hitting the shore right here in Bexley – and you get to be a part of it! It brings a tear to my eye, it does – sorry, sorry – have you got a tissue?

She moves the tinsel again –

PRIEST. To love, cherish, and obey.

Beat.

Donna, it's you.

DONNA. I'd like some time to think.

PRIEST. You don't need to think, just repeat it.

DONNA. The thing is, I've got my work.

She moves the tinsel. The sound of a crying baby.

There, there. There there. There there.

What do you want, eh?

Oh Lord. Please stop. Please stop.

OBERSTURMBANNFÜHRER. 'Please stop'? How disappointing! Where is your famous English courage? The spirit of the Vixen? But so it is, when you are at the mercy of the Thousand-Year Reich –

DONNA. You're not in this bit.

OBERSTURMBANNFÜHRER. And yet, here we are! The agents of the Reich are always one step ahead!

DONNA. Be quiet, you're waking the baby.

OBERSTURMBANNFÜHRER. Ha! Very good. But I'm afraid, you, Vixen, are in no position to be making demands. Ve have waited many years to have you at our mercy – and now, so you are – at the mercy of the Thousand-Year Reich! You know the sentence has been passed? Are you anxious to know your fate?

DONNA. Death?

OBERSTURMBANNFÜHRER. The sentence is death!

DONNA. You mustn't shout like that.

The baby's crying gets louder.

I'm coming, love, I'm coming.

There is a knocking at the door.

PETER (*off*). Donna?

DONNA. Be quiet!

OBERSTURMBANNFÜHRER. Oh ho, what's this? Some last hope of rescue? Perhaps you think your English friends will save you?

DONNA. Oh stop it!

She moves the tinsel around – the sounds fade out, leaving only the knocking at the door.

PETER. Donna? Are you decent?

DONNA. What a question! Of course I'm decent!

PETER. We're coming in okay?

PETER *and* SANDY *enter.*

DONNA. I want my money back!

PETER. What money? We haven't got your money –

DONNA *throws the tinsel at him.*

DONNA. It don't work!

PETER. I don't understand –

DONNA. Give me another one, I won't take any old tat –

PETER. I can't give you any more of this, Donna, I've got to take it away.

DONNA. But I need it! Give it back!

PETER. I'm not supposed to –

SANDY. Give it back to her.

Beat. PETER *gives* DONNA *the tinsel back.* DONNA *looks at* SANDY *suspiciously.*

PETER. Oh – this is Inspector –

SANDY. Eastwood.

DONNA. Inspector Eastwood is it?

SANDY. That's right.

DONNA. I've seen you before.

SANDY. I don't think so.

PETER. Inspector Eastwood's writing a report about us here.

DONNA. Inspection is it? Turn the place upside down, why don't you, you'll find nothing

PETER. We're not looking for anything

DONNA. You won't get it out of me, I've signed the Official
   Secrets Act.

PETER (*to* SANDY). I think we'd better come back later –

DONNA. Talking to them now! Mates with them now! We've
   got words for people like you –

PETER. What words?

DONNA. I won't say, it's not polite.

PETER. Donna, you're not making sense.

DONNA. You're not making sense! Distracting me!

PETER. Have you taken your medication?

DONNA. Why should I? I'm not sick.

PETER. We had a deal –

DONNA. Don't talk to me about deals! You lied!

   PETER *looks round the room, finds* DONNA*'s medication.*

PETER. Donna, there's four days of pills here! You have to take
   these!

DONNA. Do not.

PETER. You do, Donna! Or I'll get in trouble! (*To* SANDY.)
   I'm sorry about this –

DONNA. Look at you – mates with them now – sucking up –

PETER. What are you talking about?

DONNA. Collaborator! Turncoat! Quisling! Fink!

PETER. This is why you need to take your pills, Donna! You
   get worked up!

   He puts her medication in her hand.

   Beat.

   I've got to see you take them Donna.

SANDY. Okay. That was very good. I'll take over now.

PETER. What's that?

SANDY. Bye bye Peter. You can go now.

PETER. Um – I've got to see her take them –

SANDY. I can do it.

PETER. Um – I'm not sure –

SANDY. Peter. You've done very well. I'm going to give you a great report. I'm going to say you have exceptional imaginative capacity. As long as you go away.

Now.

PETER. But the rules say –

SANDY. But *I* say.

PETER. But –

SANDY. Peter! *Exceptional*.

PETER. Right. Right. Okay then.

He goes. DONNA *is staring at* SANDY *suspiciously.*

DONNA. Don't think – you won't make me

SANDY *takes* DONNA*'s hand and tips her pills onto the floor.*

SANDY. Come on!

DONNA. What'd he call you? Inspector Eastwood? You ain't no inspector. I know about it. I know what they do and they don't – what's your rank?

SANDY. Rank? Granny, it's me.

DONNA. Don't call me, what, what did you call me?

SANDY *opens her rucksack and takes out a large, wrapped Christmas present. She puts it in* DONNA*'s lap.*

What's this? A trap? I know that, you won't get me to

SANDY. It's not a trap, Granny, it's me! I've come to get you. They've been keeping you here, Granny. It ain't right. We need you back at home now.

DONNA. Home?

SANDY. Yeah, home.

DONNA....Sandy?

SANDY. That's right.

Beat.

DONNA. You're Daniel's girl.

SANDY. That's right!

DONNA. Oh my love –

She pulls her in for a hug.

– and I didn't recognise – I'm sorry, love – I'm so sorry – it's here, you see all sorts of things – strange things – they send 'em in to keep you muddled – keep your head mixed up. Oh Sandy, Sandy, it's you!

She goes to hug her again but SANDY *stops her.*

SANDY. We got to get moving, Gran.

DONNA. Moving?

SANDY. I've come to get you out. Look.

She goes to her bag, pulls out a big blueprint.

This is a map of this whole place.

DONNA. How'd you get this?

SANDY. Council. I said it was for school. It's all s'posed to be public anyway. They said I couldn't take anything, but I waited for the guy to go to the toilet and swapped it out for an empty tube.

DONNA. Oooh, that's good work!

SANDY. Look, Granny – we're here. Aren't we? On the second floor. So we just need to get to those stairs, and out the fire exit. I've cut through here – by the canal. We can get onto the canal and follow it back – it's only two hours – we can be there before Dad gets back.

DONNA. Dad? Your dad? He's not here –

SANDY. Course he's not here. It's a surprise.

We just need to get out of here, with no one seeing. But I think this – this here – is like a service corridor. Where it's all just plumbing and switches and that. So there won't be cameras. And we can get out.

DONNA. Out.

SANDY. That's right Granny! Get home!

DONNA. They'll notice I'm gone though – they check up on us in our rooms –

SANDY *indicates the present on* DONNA*'s lap.*

SANDY. Open it.

Merry Christmas, Granny.

DONNA *unwraps the present. It's a papier-mâché model of her head.*

5

ARDEN *and* PETER *are staring at a piece of tinsel decorating a wall.*

ARDEN. Right. No. Sorry. Tell me again.

PETER. Um. She said she was writing a report. On the whole place. And me. A whole page about me. And she said how would it look if I didn't know how to do a Christmas she said. And then she told me to put it back. So I did.

ARDEN. She said she was here to inspect everything?

PETER. Just like you said.

ARDEN. Tonight?

PETER. Yeah, tonight.

ARDEN. Did you see some ID?

PETER. You didn't say anything about asking for ID –

ARDEN. Alright, calm down, never mind.

PETER. She's really interested. Asked loads of questions. She said she'd say I displayed exceptional imaginative capacity.

ARDEN. What's that got to do with anything? Where is she now?

PETER. With Mrs Quexis.

ARDEN. Why?

PETER. She wanted to see her.

ARDEN. Why?

PETER. I don't know, she asked to see her

ARDEN. Did she talk to her?

PETER. No – not really – I was just making sure Mrs Quexis took her medication and she said it was okay and I should leave her to do it. So I did.

ARDEN. So you just left her alone with a vulnerable resident and all her medication?

PETER. Is that bad?

ARDEN. Yes it's bad! It's very obviously bad! You should have called me the minute she showed up! You haven't seen any ID, you don't even know who this person is, you've disobeyed my direct instructions just because she told you to and now you're letting a total stranger have access to the resident's medication! You've got no idea who she is! And now you're keeping me here till bloody ten at night trying to sort out your mess! And you're making me shout!

She sits down and does some breathing.

PETER. Are you okay?

ARDEN. I'm trying not to get angry.

PETER. Oh. So you're angry?

ARDEN. Of course I'm –

She stops herself, breathes again. Beat.

PETER. Can I

ARDEN. No

PETER. Cup of tea

ARDEN. THERE'S CAFFEINE IN TEA.

It's fine.

It's fine.

I'm fine.

Don't worry about me, Peter. You want to worry about yourself.

PETER. I am trying Miss Arden, I'm sorry, I'm really trying

ARDEN. Listen. It's really simple. Just – don't do anything.
Except what I tell you. Just do those things that I tell you to do.

PETER. Right.

What are you telling me to do?

ARDEN. Absolutely nothing.

She stands up.

I'm going to go talk to this woman. What's her name?

6

Split scene.

In DONNA*'s room: It's very dark. We can just see a dimly lit figure of* DONNA *sat upright in bed.*

Elsewhere: SANDY. *She talks to us from a spotlight.*

SANDY. *Escape from Alcatraz*, right, it's a true movie. It's
based on true facts. And one of the best bits is the ending.
Because no one knows what happened at the end. I mean in
real life. They got off the island but maybe they drowned.
But the way they do it in the movie is great.

There's a knock at DONNA*'s door.*

ARDEN. Inspector Eastwood?

The door opens and ARDEN *pokes her head in. Light
silhouettes her in the doorway.*

SANDY *lifts her hands into the light – she's holding
a length of electrical cable and a pair of boltcutters.
She cuts the cable.*

The light behind ARDEN *dies.* ARDEN *pointlessly flicks the switch up and down.*

SANDY. All the way through the movie, there's the warden. He's like the head screw. He's really slimy like a headteacher. And he's got this flower. A chrysanthemum. It ain't his, he stole it from Clint Eastwood's friend and now he just walks around with it, playing with it in his fingers, just to be like, 'anything you like, I can take it'. But then halfway through the movie he gets all angry, and he scrunches up the flower and throws it at Clint Eastwood. And Clint Eastwood just picks it up.

And that night they escape.

ARDEN *comes into the room.*

ARDEN. Inspector? Mrs Quexis?

SANDY. The next morning, you're on the beach on Angel Island, watching all the screws walking round looking for bodies, or clues about whether they made it or what. And everyone's saying they drowned, they must have drowned because it's *Alcatraz* – but the warden looks down, and he sees the flower. Like it's just been left there. And he asks, and they tell him no sir, chrysanthemums don't grow on this island.

And he doesn't tell anyone. But now he knows. And he'll always know it until the day he dies.

They beat him.

ARDEN *approaches the figure of* DONNA.

ARDEN. Mrs Quexis? Hello? Sorry to wake you –

There was someone here a moment ago, wasn't there? I think you spoke to her? Miss? It's quite important you tell me what she said.

ARDEN *reaches out to touch the figure.*

SANDY *touches the two cut ends of the wire together* –

The lights come on blindingly –

At ARDEN*'s touch, the figure falls apart to reveal a papier-mâché head and a pile of bedclothes.*

Blackout.

7

SANDY *and* DONNA. SANDY *leads the way, talking as she goes.*

SANDY.... And then the movie just ends. Right? You never see them again. 'Cause in real life they never got seen again so if you saw them in the movie it wouldn't be true. But you knew they made it 'cause the flower's on the beach. You see? Don't you think it's clever?

Granny?

Granny?

DONNA *has fallen behind and gotten distracted by something.* SANDY *turns around, and goes to her. Gently pulls* DONNA*'s head round to face her. They look at each other. She smiles.* DONNA *smiles.*

DONNA. Sorry love?

SANDY. Weren't you listening?

DONNA. Listening? Who are you to ask me that? Of course I was listening.

SANDY. Sorry Granny.

DONNA. The cheek to ask me that.

SANDY. We should get going.

DONNA. All I do is listen. They won't stay quiet for a minute. Try to find a moment's piece to write me book –

SANDY. Granny?

DONNA. Someone ought to keep that baby quiet!

SANDY. What baby? Granny, we're escaping. Come on.

She pulls DONNA *up. Too hard. It hurts.* DONNA *lets out a little cry.*

DONNA. Oooh!

SANDY. Sorry!

DONNA. That hurt –

SANDY. Sorry Granny –

DONNA. Don't think you can get me to talk like that! It'll take more than that!

SANDY. Granny?

DONNA. Do your worst!

SANDY. I don't want to do my worst, Granny, it's me!

DONNA. Hmm?

Oh, Sandy. Hello love.

SANDY. Do you need a little rest, Granny?

DONNA. That would be lovely.

SANDY. Okay. Just a minute. I don't want you to be Butts.

DONNA. You don't want me to be what?

SANDY. Butts. In the movie. He's the one they leave behind. He tries to dig out but he's not strong enough to make the hole. So they have to leave him. Clint Eastwood waits for as long as he can but they can't wait forever. And in the end they go without him. It's the saddest bit of the movie. That's how you can tell it's a true movie, 'cause they leave the sad bits in.

DONNA. Sounds very grown up. I wonder if it's suitable.

SANDY. It is too suitable! There's only one bit of naked when they fight in the shower, and you don't see any willies really. And one bit where Doc gets an axe and chops his fingers off. Also there's a suicide. Apart from that it's all suitable. And it's got a good message and important social values. And it's got Clint Eastwood who is the best actor in the world.

DONNA. I don't approve of violent pictures. You'll find enough violence in life.

SANDY. It's not violent, there's just two fights

DONNA. That's two too many! You ought to know that. This is the trouble with never having had a war.

SANDY. Were you in the war?

DONNA. Of course I was.

SANDY. Did you kill anyone?

DONNA. That would be telling.

SANDY. That means you did.

DONNA. You'll find it all out when the book's finished! It'll all be in the book.

SANDY. Is it nearly done?

DONNA. Very nearly. One chapter to go.

SANDY. Right. Um. Granny?

DONNA. What?

SANDY. Did you bring it?

DONNA. Course I brought it! There's top-secret information in there. You don't leave that lying about.

SANDY. Okay. So where is it?

DONNA. Where's what?

SANDY. The book.

DONNA taps her head.

DONNA. Safe up here.

SANDY. You're writing it in your head?

DONNA. Safest place. Stop anyone getting their hands on it. Get it all good and straight.

SANDY. And you remember it all?

DONNA. Course I remember it. I'm the one it all happened to. Who else is gonna remember it?

Want me to read you a bit?

SANDY. Okay!

DONNA. Right. This is about parachuting into occupied France. The second time, mind you.

Pause while DONNA collects herself. A long enough pause that we think maybe she's not going to do it. And then she recites:

'It was night. And even the stars were dark. We came in as low as we could on a plane with its wings painted black. The only light was the town behind the hills, its searchlights up to the sky, and its guns. One thousand feet. Low enough to go under their radar. But a dangerous height for a jump. It's a curious feeling, what happens to your heart between the moment you jump and the moment you pull the cord. The ground coming towards you like

Sudden deafening interruption:

OBERSTURMBANNFÜHRER. Like the forces of the Reich!!!!

And a dying fall as the sound fades away.

Beat.

SANDY. Granny?

DONNA. like

No, stop it, you're talking too much. I won't sign anything until I get a minute to think.

SANDY. Granny? That was really good –

DONNA. I said be quiet, it's my money!

SANDY. Gran?

DONNA. Well then one of them can buy it!

SANDY *takes* GRANNY*'s head in her hands again and looks at her.*

SANDY. Are you okay?

DONNA. What's that? Sandy?

What are we doing?

SANDY. You stopped.

DONNA. Stopped what?

SANDY. Stopped reading.

DONNA. This is what I've been telling you. You can't get a moment's peace.

SANDY. We'd better get moving.

DONNA. Moving?

SANDY. Yeah. We're escaping Gran.

DONNA. I knew that.

What about the others?

SANDY. What about them?

DONNA. It's a shame. To think of them all locked away. And one gets out. Doesn't seem right.

SANDY. You can't save everyone.

DONNA. Why not, though?

SANDY. Not enough heads.

8

ARDEN*'s office*. ARDEN *and* PETER.

ARDEN *is staring at the papier-mâché head*.

ARDEN. It's really quite well done. I mean it's crude but in the dark – I really thought I'd knocked her head clean off. You do worry about that, don't you, do you find? They seem so fragile. I've always had that fear, one touch and they'll fall apart.

You must have done a bit of this, mustn't you?

PETER. A bit of what?

ARDEN. Papier-mâché. Arts and crafts.

PETER. Not really, no.

ARDEN. Come on, Peter. Creative lad like you. I bet you were good at it.

PETER. I wasn't good at anything.

ARDEN. Class clown, was it? Couldn't do the work but kept everyone laughing with your funny little pranks?

PETER. No – er –

ARDEN. Come on then, where is she?

PETER. Who?

ARDEN. Mrs Quexis? You can come out now!

PETER. She's with the inspector –

ARDEN. Oh yes! The inspector! I walked into that one, didn't
I! Look out, Peter, they're sending out inspectors – what,
they're here? I really bought it! For a minute there I really
believed my own crap.

PETER. You made it up?

ARDEN. Peter, it's 10 p.m. on Christmas Eve. Do you really
think anyone cares enough to come out now? We might get
someone in the New Year, maybe. It'll be hello, how are you,
tick tick tick, take the register, are the fire exits unobstructed,
excellent, goodbye, see you in ten years. I mean do you think
anyone is really interested in what happens here? To these
people? Noticed a lot of visitors, have you? Lots of happy
families coming to gather round Granny's knee at the
weekend? Wipe the drool off her bib? This isn't that sort of
place, Peter. There are places like that. They've got nice
well-kept gardens and theatre companies coming in to do
arts workshops once a week. There's those places, and
there's these places. This is the other kind of place. You put
people here so they vanish. Pfft. Gone. And no one has to
think about them again. Except fucking me.

Now where the hell is Mrs Quexis?

PETER. She said she was – inspecting

ARDEN. Who did?

PETER. The inspector!

ARDEN. Are you screwing with me? There's really someone
here? A woman?

PETER. Well, a girl –

ARDEN. A girl? What do you mean a girl? How old is she?

PETER. Like – twelve?

ARDEN. TWELVE – FUCKING TWELVE

PETER. YOU SAID IT COULD BE ANYONE!

I'm just trying to do what I'm told. But now you're telling
me things that aren't true and I'm doing what I'm told and it
turns out I'm being told things that are wrong and now I'm
in trouble!

She said she was an inspector. She said she was writing
a report on the whole place. She said I was thorough and
imaginative. She said –

ARDEN. Peter! Shut up!

We've got to find her.

9

SANDY *and* DONNA *at the fire exit.*

SANDY. Here it is.

Granny?

Over here.

DONNA. This is it?

SANDY. This is it.

Go on. Open it.

DONNA. What about the towers?

SANDY. What towers?

DONNA. There's snipers in 'em.

SANDY. I didn't see any towers. They must be on the other side.

DONNA. And the dogs?

SANDY. I don't think there's any dogs, Granny. It's just a door.
And then a hole where I cut through the fence. And then we
follow the canal back home, Granny. That's all we have to do.

DONNA. Home?

SANDY. That's right.

DONNA. Alright.

She puts her hands on the fire-exit door.

Alright!

She pushes it open.

They step out into a perfectly silent winter night. Snow is falling.

And then an alarm goes off.

And DONNA *runs offstage.*

SANDY. Granny, wait!

She's gone! It's snowing – so much – I can't see which way she – how'd she learn to run so fast? Granny?!

And then I see her footsteps and I follow those – calling out – Granny! But she don't hear me 'cause she don't say nothing back. They're at the fence now and going along the fence – and then the snow clears and I see her – she's through the fence!

I call out – Granny!

And she looks at me!

And then the lights flash on behind us. And I hear them.

The screws are coming.

I run to the hole – the mud's slippy but it's okay – the metal's cold and rusty and it's edges are sharp – cut myself a bit pushing through but it's okay – I'm coming Gran – I'm coming –

I'm –

I'm stuck!

My coat's caught on the wires! Can't get it off!

And I can hear them coming

And Granny's coming over, trying to pull me through but it won't work, there's no time Gran –

And I know what to do.

I take Granny's hands off where she's trying to get me free.

And I put my hands on her shoulders.

And I push her.

And I tell her –

Go.

And she goes.

When they leave Butts, they have to. If they waited for him
they'd all get caught. Butts knows they can't wait. He knows.
Sometimes one person has to sacrifice themselves. So another
one can escape. That's just how it works sometimes.

PETER *runs on, breathless.*

PETER. You

SANDY *launches herself at him.*

10

PETER *and* SANDY.

The alarm, a little quieter, is still going in the background.

SANDY *is tied to a chair.*

PETER*'s hand is bandaged. He has her rucksack.*

PETER. So. You're not really an inspector.

I didn't really think you were. I was just playing along
because I didn't want to make you look stupid. Who'd
believe you were an inspector? You're just a kid. Obviously.
If I thought you were an inspector that'd make me some kind
of, of idiot, wouldn't it? And I'm not. Obviously.

Who are you? What are you doing here?

If you don't tell me I'll find out anyway. You might as well just tell me. It'll be easier for you if you tell me now, before my boss comes. She's really smart. You're gonna be in so much trouble if she gets here and you haven't told me.

No?

You want to be in trouble?

Well fine.

He opens her bag.

What's this then? What have we here, mystery girl?

He pulls out a length of rope.

What's this for?

No answer. He goes into the bag. Takes out the blueprint.

Where'd you get this?

No answer. He goes into the bag. Pulls out some boltcutters.

And these?

SANDY *says nothing.* PETER *tries to hide it but he's a bit freaked out.*

What are you supposed to be? A spy? Is this – *Spy Kids*? That's what I'm meant to think, is it? *Spy Kids* is real?

SANDY *says nothing. He goes back to the bag, rummages in it. Pulls out a mobile phone.*

Ah-hah!

Not so smart now, are you? Now I've got this?

Suppose I call your parents?

Would you like that? Your parents find out where you are? What you've been doing? Fine then.

He tries to use the phone. The screen is locked.

What's the code?

Look, you're in a lot of trouble, you know. Real trouble.

If I can't call your parents I'm calling the police. Okay? You understand? You've committed a crime – you've committed a lot of crimes. You're a criminal, that's what you are now. They'll put you in prison. You understand that? Would you like that? To go to prison? What would you do if they put you in prison?

SANDY. Escape.

PETER. No you wouldn't! You can't just escape from things! When they put you somewhere you have to stay there or they put you somewhere worse! That's how it is!

ARDEN enters.

ARDEN. Peter, what are you doing? This is a child, you can't just tie her to a chair!

PETER. She bit me!

ARDEN. I don't care if she bit you, it's not okay, you can't treat children like that, there are laws about it! Untie her!

He unties her.

And go and see if you can shut that alarm off. It's woken the whole place up, it's chaos out there.

He goes.

So. Hello.

I'm Arden. I run this place.

What's your name?

SANDY. Eastwood.

ARDEN. Well. Good to meet you. Eastwood.

How old are you?

SANDY. Eleven.

ARDEN. That's terrifying.

I hope you realise what you've done here, Eastwood. You've kidnapped an old, vulnerable woman.

SANDY. She's not kidnapped.

ARDEN. No? What is she then?

SANDY. Escaped.

ARDEN. Escaped? This isn't a prison, Eastwood, it's a care home. We're not keeping her here against her will. We're looking after her. Because she can't look after herself.

What do you think? You've spent some time with her. Did she strike you as someone who could look after herself? I realise I don't know her like you know her. But I work here, I see her every day. And, I mean, bright woman, sure. Energetic, certainly. But I wouldn't say she's got what I call a firm grip on reality.

And she's old.

And it's cold.

And she's by the canal.

Aren't you a bit worried?

SANDY. You're trying to scare me.

ARDEN. I'm trying to make you realise, you've put her in a lot of danger.

SANDY. She's been in a war! She dropped into France on a parachute and killed Nazis! She's done more cool stuff than you'll ever do in your whole life!

ARDEN. Eastwood, Mrs Quexis is eighty-four years old. That means when the war started she was nine. I don't know what she's told you but I very much doubt she's killed anyone.

The alarm stops.

SANDY *is upset.*

Look, don't cry. It's not too late. We can still help her. You just need to help us. What's your real name, love?

SANDY. Sandy.

ARDEN. Is she your granny, Sandy?

SANDY *nods.*

Don't worry, okay? There's plenty of time for us to find her.
She won't have got far. Then we'll bring her back, and keep
her safe. That's what we do here. We look after people.

We're professionals at it.

PETER *enters*.

PETER. I got the alarm.

ARDEN. Yes, thank you, we noticed.

This is Sandy, Peter.

Sandy's just about to call her parents and ask them to come
collect her.

PETER. Oh. Okay.

Um. Are you busy?

ARDEN. Why?

PETER. It's just, some of the residents are a bit agitated –

ARDEN. What's happened

PETER. I think the alarm going off's upset them – they're
worried there's a burglar –

ARDEN. Well tell them there isn't a burglar!

PETER. I did but – Mrs Connolly's got a posse together and
they're going room to room –

ARDEN. Oh god

PETER. I think they need you to talk to them.

ARDEN. Why me?

PETER. You're the manager.

Pause. ARDEN *stops herself from swearing.*

ARDEN. Fine. You stay here. With her. Until her parents come.
Got it?

You do not move.

PETER. Got it.

ARDEN. I'll be back as soon as I can, Sandy.

ARDEN *goes.*

Silence.

SANDY. What's going to happen to Granny?

PETER. Oh – she'll be okay. She's pretty smart. And Miss
Arden's really smart, she'll find her soon anyway. I'm sure
she'll be fine.

SANDY. She's not crazy!

PETER. I didn't say she was

SANDY. Is she?

PETER. I don't

SANDY. She is though, isn't she.

She thought there were guard towers with snipers in them.

PETER. Yeah, we don't have those.

Are you going to call your parents?

SANDY. You do it.

She unlocks the screen, gives him the phone.

He won't pick up.

He calls. No answer.

Told you.

PETER. What about your mum?

SANDY. Don't have her number.

Beat.

Why do you work here?

PETER. I've got to work, I had an assessment.

SANDY. But why here? Is it a good place?

PETER. What do you mean?

SANDY. Do people like being here?

PETER. Sometimes. Some of them. I don't know.

SANDY. She wanted to go.

PETER. Yeah.

SANDY. So it must have been bad. If it's a bad place you shouldn't work here. Good people shouldn't work in a bad place. Why do you do it?

PETER. Your granny, did she ever tell you about penny luck?

SANDY. What's that?

PETER. Find a penny, pick it up, all day long you'll have good luck. You didn't know about that?

SANDY. No.

PETER. I just wondered if it was an all-grannies thing.

SANDY. You've got a granny?

PETER. Yes. Except she died.

She used to look after me while Mum was working. She was a waitress so her hours were all over. So I'd stay with Granny till she finished work. She'd tell me about penny luck and karma and things like that.

SANDY. Karma?

PETER. Yeah, you know. It means when you do good things, good things happen to you. And when you do bad things, bad things happen to you. You get back what you give out.

SANDY. Is that true?

PETER. No, it's not. I tested it.

'Cause pennies – when you find pennies on the ground, right, where do they come from? People drop them. Then you find them. And then they give you luck. So that means the person dropping the penny is doing something good. Right? 'Cause they're giving you something. So that means they should get karma. So you get luck, and they get karma, and everyone wins, right? It goes up for everyone. 'Cause luck and karma are sort of the same. So if finding a penny is lucky, and dropping a penny is lucky, everyone ought to be going around dropping pennies and picking them up again and getting luckier and luckier. Right?

SANDY. Right.

PETER. But no one was trying it. Everyone I knew went around
keeping all their money in their wallets and not giving it to
anyone, no wonder they never had any. So I got the jar where
Mum kept the Christmas money and I took it to the shop and
changed it into pennies. Had to go to a lot of shops a lot of
times but in the end I had the jar filled up, right? Big glass jar,
as big as your head, all filled up with pennies, right to the brim.
And then I took that out onto the balcony outside the flat. And
I sat on it and waited. Some of the other kids saw me but it was
funny, no one tried to nick it, even though they would if it'd
been notes. But I guess a jar of pennies doesn't seem quite like
money. Like, it's money, but it's something else too, isn't it?
Maybe it's all the luck. So I just sat on the jar and waited till
the sun went down. And then I saw Mum. She was walking
over the courtyard to our block. So I stood up on the edge and
shouted MUM until she saw me and then I pushed the jar off
the edge and it went SMASH and that's when all the kids
started legging it, legging it down the stairs to pick up the
pennies, filling their pockets with them and just throwing them
around like it was snow. But Mum just stood there. Looking up
at me. And I thought, pick them up, pick them up Mum,
you've got to pick them up, or you won't get the luck. Or the
money. And we'll all be worse off instead of better. But she
just looked at me like she didn't understand. And when she
came upstairs she gave Granny a hiding and not long after that
she was gone. And when Granny died they moved me into
care. And I sort of blamed Gran for it, a bit, 'cause she'd given
me the idea. But that's not fair, is it? She just had some wrong
ideas. It was me that went with them. So that's not her fault.
It's my fault for getting the wrong ideas.

I was really hoping you were an inspector, you know. 'Cause
if there was an inspector they could just come along, tell you
what was the right thing, and what wasn't. And what you
should do to sort it all out. There should be someone whose
job it is to sort things out like that.

Do you know which way your granny was going?

SANDY. Yeah. I saw her running.

PETER. And you think you can find her?

SANDY. Yes.

PETER. Okay.

PETER gives SANDY her bag back.

I'm going to go now.

SANDY. But she told you to stay with me –

PETER. Yeah but. I'm going to go I think. Miss Arden'll need help getting people back in their rooms.

I'm locking the door, okay?

SANDY. But –

PETER. If it gets stuffy, you can open the window. It's not locked.

SANDY. Thank you.

PETER. Good luck.

He goes.

SANDY stands up.

She goes to the window and opens it.

A blast of cool air.

SANDY. Cold. It's even colder now. But it's not a big jump like before.

I run across to the hole in the fence. There's bits of her nightie stuck to the edges of the hole where it tore. It's still snowing a bit and the footprints are getting covered but you can still see them. So I follow them down the canal. It's dark still and there's still people. You can't see them but you can feel them, watching, in the bushes like before. And there's a lot of mud like the snow's melted –

and it's slippy –

and it's dark –

my granny is clever! She *did* fight in a war! She knows how to find her way in the dark without no compass, and she was nine years old when she killed her first Nazi, and I am her granddaughter and she is not not not not not not *not* going in the canal –

She's not –

She's just *not*.

I won't *let* her.

And then the footprints just – stop.

Lights come up around SANDY, *standing by the edge of the canal.*

G – Granny?

An awful silence.

And then:

Splash! We hear someone diving into the water. Pulling something onto the bank. The stage is flooded with blinding light.

CLINT EASTWOOD *enters – grizzled, forties, wearing the blue shirt and grey trousers uniform of Alcatraz. He is soaking wet and carries an equally soaking* DONNA *in his arms.*

He lays her down and pumps water from her lungs.

He breathes life into her mouth.

She coughs. Wakes.

CLINT EASTWOOD *leans down and whispers something in* DONNA*'s ear. They both look up at* SANDY.

CLINT EASTWOOD *holds out his hand to her. On his palm is a yellow chrysanthemum flower.* SANDY *takes it.*

Blackout.

11

DONNA *is alone onstage.*

She is soaking wet and her legs are caked in mud.

A new voice speaks – very posh, British, clipped, male.

OFFICER. Donna? We need you to sign.

DONNA. What?

OFFICER. All the others have signed it.

DONNA. What'm I signing?

OFFICER. It's the Official Secrets Act, Donna.

It's an understanding between you and Her Majesty's government. That the work you do here will be shared with no one. That you will never speak of it. That when the work is done you will return to your life as it was and say nothing. Husband. Son. Marriage. That will be your life. The work you have done with us, the things you have accomplished, your great adventure – of that, you will remain silent.

DONNA. I can't tell them?

OFFICER. That's right.

DONNA. Why not?

OFFICER. Because we want you girls to live a normal life. Sign here.

DONNA. I don't want to –

OFFICER. I'm afraid it's compulsory. Part of the deal.

The sound of a baby crying begins to play.

DONNA. Daniel?

OFFICER. I'm sorry?

DONNA. Daniel, don't cry love –

OFFICER. I need your signature, Donna.

DONNA. I don't know about that.

OFFICER. You have to sign it.

DONNA. I don't want to –

The OFFICER*'s voice begins to shift, develop a German accent – becomes –*

OBERSTURMBANNFÜHRER. But you vill have to, Vixen, if you wish to get out off here alive.

DONNA. Leave me alone.

OBERSTURMBANNFÜHRER. Leave you alone? It is too late for zat, Vixen! Perhaps it is you who should have left well alone! For if you had not been so foolish, you could have had a happy life. But instead, look at you now. Alone and dying – in a dark cell – with death approaching. And for what? For an *adventure*. Was it worth it, Vixen? Was it worth challenging the might of ZE THIRD REICH

SANDY *enters. She is holding some towels.*

DONNA. Don't shout like that –

OBERSTURMBANNFÜHRER. YOU VILL NOT STOP ME SHOUTING

DONNA. You'll wake the baby

OBERSTURMBANNFÜHRER. ZE BABY IS AWAKE!

DONNA. Daniel – there there, Daniel – it's alright love –

OBERSTURMBANNFÜHRER. VILL YOU SIGN?

DONNA. Go away

OBERSTURMBANNFÜHRER. YOU MUST SIGN IT DONNA!

DONNA. I won't! I won't sign it!

The crying stops.

OBERSTURMBANNFÜHRER. Well. It matters not, Vixen. No one will believe you.

SANDY. Granny?

DONNA. They will! Why shouldn't they!

SANDY. Shh, Granny, it's okay Gran –

DONNA. Daniel –

SANDY. No, Granny, it's me – Sandy.

DONNA. Sandy?

She looks at her. Recognises her.

Sandy!

You've come to get me out! Quickly – while there's still time – let's go –

She tries to get up out of the chair. SANDY *stops her.*

SANDY. No Granny we've done that. We're home.

DONNA. Home?

She looks around her. The lights fade up around her and we see where we are: in SANDY*'s front room. A TV, an armchair, a spartan Christmas tree, a mince pie and a glass of brandy. The TV is on and a movie is playing.*

This is home?

SANDY. That's right. But we got to stay quiet. Dad's asleep.

Are you hungry?

She offers DONNA *the mince pie.*

It's s'posed to be for Father Christmas but he's not real. He's just Dad really. And Dad won't mind. Do you want it?

DONNA. 'Scold.

SANDY. How about a drink?

She offers DONNA *the brandy. Tries to help her drink it.* DONNA *spits it out.*

Sorry!

I'll clean you up –

She starts to wipe DONNA *up and dry her off.* DONNA *is shivering.*

You cold Granny?

DONNA *nods.*

You'll soon warm up. It'll be okay.

DONNA *is staring at the TV.*

DONNA. Who's that?

SANDY. That? That's him.

DONNA. This is –

SANDY. The best movie in the world. I put it on for you. Here.

She turns the volume up. DONNA *watches* Escape from Alcatraz *while* SANDY *dries her off with the towels.*

This is a good bit.

There he is. See? Look at that.

He's so good.

He looks taller in the movie don't he? That's how you know he's a good actor 'cause he looks bigger. I guess no one can be as big in real life as they can in a movie.

Granny?

What did he say to you?

DANIEL *enters in his dressing gown. He is played by the same actor who played* CLINT EASTWOOD.

He stares at the two of them watching the film.

DANIEL. Mum?

He turns the TV off and puts the lights on. Blinding, glaring.

Sandy? What's going on? Why's she here?

SANDY. She's come back for Christmas.

DANIEL. 'Sthat… Mum, you can't just turn up like this, Mum. Why didn't they tell me they were letting you out?

DONNA. They dint let me out –

DANIEL. Jesus, it's nearly midnight and you just turn up out of the blue, don't even ask or anything, this is just like you –

SANDY. It's okay Dad

DANIEL. Don't tell me it's okay! You can't do things like that, Sandy!

DONNA. Don't shout –

SANDY. It's okay Gran

DANIEL. Don't shout? Don't shout? That's rich from you, Mum, never remember you minding a bit of shouting!

Jesus, you're soaked. Why's she so wet, Sandy?

SANDY. I'm just drying her –

DANIEL. You put her in that chair? That's actual leather. Come on Mum, let's get you up –

He goes to lift her up. DONNA *strikes him.*

DONNA. Get your hands off me! You can't make me talk!

DANIEL *is speechless.* SANDY *grabs him before he can get angry.*

SANDY. It's alright Dad – she's just a bit tired –

DANIEL. You don't touch me like that Mum. You've got no fucking right to touch me like that.

DONNA. Stop crying –

DANIEL. I want you gone now. I'm calling a taxi.

SANDY. No, Dad –

DANIEL *gets his phone, turns it on. It starts beeping.*

DANIEL. Thirty missed calls? What the hell's going on Sandy?

DANIEL *starts listening to his messages.*

This is the bloody police on here!

SANDY. I just wanted Granny home

for Christmas

so it wouldn't be

shit.

I did it, Dad. I got her out.

And now you're ruining it again.

DANIEL *looks at the head.*

DANIEL. Jesus, Sandy.

That's what this is about?

SANDY. Can she stay?

DANIEL. You know what I'm going to say to that.

SANDY. Say yes.

Beat.

DANIEL. Tell you what, Sandy. Close your eyes.

She closes her eyes.

He produces a parcel wrapped in brown paper and hands it to her. She feels it.

SANDY. What is it –

DANIEL. It's a present. Have a look.

She opens her eyes. Inspects it.

Read the label.

She does. Her eyes light up.

SANDY. It's from Mum!

DANIEL. That's right.

SANDY. You saw her?

DANIEL. No – Sandy – come on. You know that's not allowed. She posted it.

SANDY *inspects it.*

SANDY. There's no stamp –

DANIEL. Oh, isn't there? She must have delivered it by hand then.

SANDY. That means she's close!

DANIEL. Could do, yeah, could mean that, maybe.

SANDY. Was there a card?

DANIEL. Just that.

SANDY *goes to open it.*

Hey!

It's not Christmas yet.

SANDY. Maybe she'll come for Christmas.

DANIEL. Yeah – she won't, Sandy. You shouldn't get your hopes up for things like that.

The doorbell rings.

DANIEL *goes to open it.*

It's ARDEN.

ARDEN. Hello.

Beat.

We have met before, actually. I'm the manager at Canalside. Your mother's home?

DANIEL. Oh right, yeah.

ARDEN. Is she here?

DANIEL. Yeah, she's over there –

ARDEN. Oh thank god.

DANIEL. Yeah, I remember you. What are you doing letting my mum out this time of night?

ARDEN. I didn't let her –

DANIEL. Well, she's here.

ARDEN. Yes. Well, I'm very sorry about that. It's been – a – challenging evening.

Hello, Sandy.

SANDY *says nothing.*

DANIEL. Say hi to the lady, Sandy.

ARDEN. It's alright. The important thing is, she's safe. They're both safe. You've called an ambulance?

DANIEL. An ambulance? What for?

ARDEN. What for? For – for your mother.

DANIEL. She's alright. You're alright, aren't you Mum?

ARDEN. Alright? She's not alright! She's eighty-four years old and she just fell in the canal – of course she's not alright!

ARDEN *goes to* DONNA, *checks her pulse*.

DANIEL. The canal? You didn't say anything about the canal, Sandy –

ARDEN. Well how do you think she got like this?!

DANIEL. I don't know, I just thought – I don't know what I thought –

ARDEN. Of course not! Of course you don't! Don't you people ever *think*!

Have you even been up to us since you dropped your mother off? I've been looking after Donna for eighteen months now, you don't have the first idea who I am! I could be a serial killer for all you care! I've got three hundred residents up in that home, we could be harvesting their organs, not one of you lot would make a peep. Just so long as you don't have to think about it. Just so long as it's me and my staff doing all the wiping, the feeding, doing all the stuff you should be doing, and they hate us for it 'cause every time they look at us, they think of you lot who should be doing it instead. I'm leaving tomorrow and I won't look back once.

Yes you should call an ambulance!

DANIEL *dials 999*.

DANIEL. Hello? Ambulance please. Yes – it's me mother – she fell in the canal – no we're at home –

Yeah she's –

No – no she's not

He says to try and wake her.

ARDEN. Donna?

SANDY. Granny?

DANIEL. She's not waking up – she's not – yeah she's breathing – yeah she's – she's breathing yeah she's –

eighty-four.

Is she awake?

ARDEN. Can you hear me Donna?

DANIEL. Wake her up, come on!

ARDEN. I don't – I don't know – it wasn't me who –

Sandy?

They're asking how long she was in the water.

Sandy?

How long was she under –

Sandy!

SANDY. I don't know

DANIEL. Sandy love, please, it's important

SANDY. I didn't see her – didn't see her go in I just

just saw him save her

he saved her

Clint Eastwood saved her

DANIEL. Sandy, this isn't the time

SANDY. He did – he came running out of the bushes and –

he did it –

he saved her!

It was him! Look!

She shows DANIEL *the chrysanthemum flower.*

He looks at it for a moment and then throws it away.

DANIEL. Sandy, I'm just asking how long she was in the water.

SANDY. I – I don't know. I didn't see.

DANIEL. We don't know.

Okay – okay yes.

It's 41 Rochester Drive.

Okay.

He hangs up.

Eight minutes, they said –

they said we should keep her warm –

ARDEN. Have you got any more blankets?

DANIEL. Here.

ARDEN. Okay. Let's get her warm.

> ARDEN *and* DANIEL *start warming* DONNA *up.*
> SANDY *watches, helpless.*

SANDY. Will she be okay?

ARDEN. I hope so, Sandy.

SANDY. Where are they gonna take her?

ARDEN. To a hospital.

SANDY. And after that?

ARDEN. I don't know.

SANDY. Are they gonna take her back to that place?

ARDEN. That's not up to me.

SANDY. Who's it up to?

> Dad?

> Dad, I think she should come back here.

DANIEL. Not now, Sandy.

SANDY. She should stay with us.

DANIEL. She can't.

SANDY. Why not? Why'd you have to be so mean?

> I don't care why you're angry. She's your mum. And now
> she's back. If my mum came back I wouldn't be angry or
> anything. I'd just be happy 'cause she'd be back.

DANIEL. It's not that simple, love.

SANDY. It is. It is that simple.

> SANDY *picks up the present from her mum off the floor. She
> goes and offers it to* DONNA.

> Granny? Here, Granny. It's for you.

DANIEL. Hey now, don't do that

SANDY. I don't want it

DANIEL. That's from your mum!

SANDY. Well she's not here is she! And Granny is. It's my present so I can do what I like with it. Granny? Here.

She tries to get her to open it.

DANIEL. Love, I don't think she can

SANDY. I'll do it for her.

SANDY *opens the present. It's an exercise book, and a pen. She looks at it.*

ARDEN. Well... that's sweet.

SANDY. She's left the price on.

SANDY *looks at it. A crap present.*

DANIEL. Look, love... it's the thought that counts, you know? Don't worry about this one. You've got more presents... tomorrow we'll get up first thing and open them all, okay? There's plenty of stuff. Great stuff.

DONNA. Give it.

SANDY. Granny?

DONNA. Give it here.

DONNA *gestures for the book. Tries to take it.* SANDY *gives it to her.*

The voice comes in very loud. Only DONNA *can hear it.*

OFFICER. That's right. Sign here.

DONNA. I ain't signin'.

OFFICER. But you've got to –

DONNA. I'm writin' a book –

She tries to write in it, but her hands are too weak and she's shaking too much. She can't.

SANDY. Wait, Granny. Let me.

SANDY *takes it back off her. Sits beside her.*

OFFICER. You can't

OBERSTURMBANNFÜHRER. You can't

PRIEST. You can't

ESTATE AGENT. You can't

SANDY. Come on Granny. Tell me.

DONNA *leans in. Starts to speak.* SANDY *takes dictation.*

DONNA. I look back on my life and it seems wrong somehow.
The things I remember don't have the right weight. Like the
day you were born. That ought to be heavy. But it's like
breath on a glass. And other things feel so real. The skies
over France. And pulling the cord. And the ground coming
up at me so fast. It was night. And even the stars were dark.
We came in as low as we could on a plane with its wings
painted black…

She coughs. Her voice is going. SANDY *leans in closer.*
DONNA *whispers the book to* SANDY *and* SANDY *writes.*

COLLAPSIBLE

Margaret Perry

To my friends and family,
who keep me sane

MARGARET PERRY

Margaret Perry is a playwright from Cork, living in London.
Her first play *Porcelain* was produced by the Abbey Theatre,
Dublin, in 2018 and adapted for BBC Radio 4. She is currently
under commission to The Yard and the Bush. *Collapsible* was
developed with the kind support of an MGC Futures Bursary.

Collapsible was first performed at VAULT Festival, London, on 13 February 2019, with the following cast:

ESSIE	Breffni Holahan
Director	Thomas Martin
Designer	Alison Neighbour
Producer	Ellie Keel

It takes a village – thank you to mine: Jessi Stewart, Deirdre O'Halloran, Louise Stephens, Gillian Greer, Hannah Hauer-King, Eleanor Crosswell, Ellen Buckley, Thomas Martin, Ellie Keel, Stella McCabe and MGC Futures.

M.P.

'...a woman who lived well, lived well, lived well, lived on the uppermost layer of the sands of the world, and the sands had never caved in beneath her feet... [until] without warning, there was the loud sound of something solid that suddenly crumbles.'

The Passion According to G.H.,
Clarice Lispector

Character

ESSIE, *a woman*

Some Notes on Production

This is a piece for one actor playing one character. We see all
the other characters through Essie recalling them for us. I have
included quite a lot of 'I say' and 'she/he says' lines that I think
make the piece clearer to read, but many of these won't be
necessary in performance. If it's clear who's speaking, cut them.

*** indicates scene transitions which should be marked with
sound, or movement, or both.

ESSIE. I spend a lot of time on the internet. Especially lately.

There's this video I've watched over and over again, of this 1950s housewife on LSD. Back then they were doing clinical trials on humans, and this housewife, meek and shy as they come, has volunteered, and they've chosen her because she's undergone psychological testing and been found to be a stable, normal person. This doctor sits her down and explains everything and gives her a glass of water with a tiny measure of lysergic acid in it. She drinks it down and he waits a bit and then starts to ask her questions. And there's this one moment – this one – this one moment that I can't forget where he says, 'Mary, how do you feel?' And she says, 'I don't understand the question.' And he points to her and says, 'How do *you* feel?' And she smiles this serene smile. 'Why, doctor,' she says, 'There is no *me*. There is no *you*.' Like it's the most obvious thing in the entire world. And she looks so happy, so light.

And that's where the video ends but I always imagine her when the LSD wears off, putting on her coat and her scarf like ballast, trying to weigh herself back down.

***

It started like this. I lost my job. Not my fault. I just. Anyway. Never mind.

My sister had arranged to meet me for dinner and I knew it was because Mum had asked her to check up on me, but I went anyway to prevent further questions, and also because, food. She'd brought The Boyfriend. I'd not ordered very much because it was unclear if they were going to pay for my meal or if I was. I was eating it very slowly so as not to reveal how small it was and Maura said, are you not hungry Essie, and I said not really which was a lie, I'm always hungry, my metabolism could enter the Olympics if there was a category for metabolisms which of course, there isn't.

So Essie. What's going on with you?

Not much.

Mum says you haven't been answering her calls.

I've been really busy.

Right.

She chews. Swallows.

Anyway, I just wanted to check in, see if you're alright?

Pause.

Look up at her worried face and that's when I said it, I don't know what possessed me to say it but I said:

I feel like a chair.

Long pause.

The Boyfriend, Derek he's called, she's had him surgically attached to her, stares at his menu even though we ordered ages ago.

What's that? You feel like what?

Eh –

A chair?

Never mind, I just –

Like, that chair, there?

She points to a nearby empty chair, dark wood, a trendy, aloof chair.

Not exactly like that one, no.

Derek's listening now. I can't look at his punchable face.

What – sort of chair, then, is it that you feel like?

Like, one of those folding chairs, you know?

She thinks. She's trying, and for a moment, I love her.

A deckchair.

Not a deckchair.

Right. I mean, does the type of chair really – ?

She's shrinking back from me.

More like, you know, sort of a garden – chair?

A sun lounger?

One of those chairs you can fold and unfold. I say. Those collapsible chairs. Solid one minute and then.

The stretch of table between her and me widens and deepens into a canyon.

Now she's looking at the menu but Derek's looking at me. Her hand on his wrist, wrapped tight as his watch.

Derek, would you please get the bill.

He's staring at me.

Derek!

Mmm, he says, yeah. He turns for a waiter.

They pay for my tiny meal. I wish I'd known. I'd have had steak.

***

It started like this.

I don't remember the interviewer's face but I do remember his dry mouth peeling open to push the words out:

So, Esther.

He licked his lips, like I might be delicious.

Could you tell me briefly why you left your last job?

People said I was a fool, that I'd done well to land a permanent position in a company people the world over would kill to work for. Hammering down the doors, they were, making work for the cleaners who started two hours earlier than everyone else, polishing their handprints off the glass in the foyer. Did I think I was too good for it? Didn't I like the free fruit baskets? I certainly ate them, didn't I. I certainly ate them. I'd moved to the company from a smaller, more traditional office and I thought it would be an exciting new start. A free gym! Pizza Fridays! But I soon realised that it was the same kind of churning nothing, except now in an office designed so I could live in it, specifically designed so I never needed to go home. And then I almost missed my old work, where no one tried to make me feel special or necessary but just let me get on with it and leave at 5 p.m. sharp.

But I stuck at it, because I have been taught never to give up on anything. We love you Esther, they said. Keep doing what you're doing, but do it more. I stuck at it, the weeks rolling on like the cakes for people's birthdays. Do it more and more and more and we'll pay you more. Here's a big smile. Here's a small pay rise. The never-ending parade of cakes passing inexorably until I'd been there five years and catching sight of my face in the mirror was like seeing an old friend from school that you really meant to stay in touch with.

I was ready for a change. I say.

Well, a change is as good as a rest!

I think about closing my eyes, just for a moment. Curling up somewhere soft and small.

So Esther, he says. Why don't you tell me a little bit about yourself.

And he waited, and I realised that I hadn't prepared this question.

Myself.

Yes. Who you are, you know. What you're like.

And then this, this seam in the room ripped open and in it was a chasm of silence, a sort of, ravine, of silence, and I fell down into it and as I fell my body twisted around so that I was looking up at the shard of light at the top – and over the edge was his head, staring down at me and saying my name.

Esther? Excuse me? Could you please answer the question?

***

I'm being overly nonchalant. I'm worried Liz will notice. She doesn't. Liz tells me about the new couch she's ordered from Sweden where they really know about design. She tells me about a holiday she's booking with her most recent squeeze, someone called Hayley who works in travel so she's getting them a great deal on one of those hotels where you just press a button and a person appears holding a cocktail.

What's that smell, Liz?

Fennel and Cracked Sea Salt, she says solemnly, gesturing to a huge candle burning in the window.

Wow, I say.

It's this new thing I've started doing. I buy myself something nice once a week, something I don't really need, that's just for me. With the world the way it is, I think it's really important to practise self-care, don't you?

I –

Are you taking care of yourself, Essie?

Course.

Good. It's so important to make time to do something for you. Get a pedicure. Have a bath. It all matters. It's all political, isn't it.

Political?

Yes. How we live, it's politicised, of course it is.

Leave it, I think, leave it but then –

What political statement does having a bath make?

What?

I just mean, don't you think that's a bit convenient? Doing something for yourself, and saying it's political? Buying something, and saying it's political? So that you don't have to actually do anything real in the world, for other people?

Pause.

Do you have to shit on literally everything, Essie?

Pause.

I am trying to live a good life and be happy, alright? You're not exactly out there saving babies either, are you?

I shake my head.

Sorry.

She looks at me.

It's okay.

She says it in that virtuous way people always say that these days, like, I-know-you-are-having-a-hard-time-so-I-will-cut-you-some-slack-because-I-am-a-good-person. She moves protectively towards the fennel candle, and blows it out. I'm not worthy of its majesty.

I've known Liz my whole life and I sometimes think we are only friends now because we have been friends for so long. But she knows me. She knows me and that is – I want to hang on to that.

Liz. I've got a question for you.

Fire away, she says.

What do you think I'm like?

What?

Like if someone asked you, oh, what's Essie like –

Yeah?

What would you say?

I dunno, she says. Come on, Es, you know what you're like.

Course, I say carefully. Course I do. But I have to, sell myself, you know, for my job applications, and I'm running out of things to say. So I've decided to make a list. Crowdsource it from people who know me.

She pauses.

YES, she says.

What?

YES! I like it. It's innovative, it's proactive. You're taking control, Es. I'm happy for you.

Pause.

I'd say you were practical. No-nonsense, she says,
a no-nonsense girl with your feet firmly on the ground.

Thanks.

Anything to help you with the job hunt.

How are you – managing?

She whispers this.

I have all the money I saved for the trip.

I was going to go travelling. A year-long holiday. But we didn't call it that, she and I. We called it an adventure. We're going on an adventure, we'd say to each other, bouncing flights and hostels and guided tours and city maps back and forth between us in snatched moments between meetings and from laptop to laptop side by side in bed. Holidays were for other people; other people went on holiday; but we had adventures.

When I get home, I open a fresh page of my notebook. I write my name on the top of the page and underneath it I write –

Practical. No-Nonsense.

I look at the words on the page. I close my eyes and try to picture myself. All I can see is the blur of eyelids. Mine, I think.

***

It's nice to see you.

What do you want?

Jack's lips are a disc-drive slit.

Oh I –

You ghost me months ago and now you suddenly want a coffee?

Eh. Yeah.

Bit fucking rude.

You're here though. I say.

Only out of morbid curiosity.

Thanks.

You dropped off the face of the earth. Thought you might've died.

Right, I say, well, sorry to disappoint. I'll get right to it.
No-Nonsense.

I take out the list.

I'm making a list of words that describe me.

And since you know me pretty well – used to, I mean,
I wondered if you had anything to add to it. He looks at it.

Fuck's this?

It's just – research, I say, for my interviews.

You're getting interviews then?

Yeah, I say. Tons.

That's good, he says in a really angry voice.

So can you help me out?

Pause.

You're a militant perfectionist, he says. But don't tell them
that's your greatest weakness, they've heard that a million
times. Have you got a weakness prepared?

I'm in the process of choosing one from the platter. He
laughs like you might laugh at the joke of an elderly relative,
and sort of pats my arm.

He looks at the list again.

This is really weird, Essie, he says.

Nah, it's just – something to keep me busy.

Why can't you just binge-watch a series like a normal person.

Pause.

You need to get your shit together, sharpish.

Pause.

I have to wee, I reply.

In the bathroom I touch the skin on my cheek and it feels
like somebody else's skin.

***

Can't get the sliver of it out of my head. The way she used to look at me when I came home at the end of a day. I don't miss anything about her except for that. And you can get that with a dog, too. The way they look up when you come through the door.

I sometimes imagine that I'll have an accident and be rushed to the hospital and while they're operating, dramatically you know just a team of people all standing around me, most of them not really doing very much, sort of just there for effect even though the hospital is chronically understaffed and groaning at the seams with all the bodies it contains in various stages of broken – while they're operating, someone will ask, in low tones so you know it's important – 'Who's the next of kin?' and someone else will produce my NHS registration form and right down at the bottom it'll say 'Andrea Bones.' 'We need to get in touch with Ms Bones IMMEDIATELY' the senior surgeon will say, one hand inside my chest cavity, gesticulating wildly with the other.

And someone will go and call the number I've written down and at home in my flat on my kitchen table my phone will start to vibrate and from the living room Andrea will raise her head off her paws and pad softly into the kitchen to stand under the table, confused, trying to locate the source of the sound.

***

I'm watching my dad eat a kebab.

Very good-quality meat in this, Esther. Do you want a bite?

No thanks.

Very nice place this. Very friendly staff.

No need to sound so surprised.

What are these green things?

Peppers.

They're very nice.

I'm glad Dad. What time's your train tonight?

Seven, he says. I've only just got here and you're already counting down the minutes till you can get rid of me!

He wipes his mouth.

How're your job applications going, love?

I've got an interview on Friday.

Oh I'm so relieved! He says. Give it your all, won't you.

Yeah Dad, I will.

Give it everything you got.

I will.

I mean it now. Go into that room with absolutely everything you've got.

He lowers his voice.

Are you – you know – managing? Financially?

Yeah. I'm okay.

He exhales.

Well that's good to hear! Because – well I must say –

What?

When you said you wanted to meet up, your mother and I – well I thought you might need money.

Because that's the only reason I'd ever want to see you, is it.

Course not love. Course not! Just you sounded urgent, on the phone, you sounded – not quite yourself.

Oh?

I was worried. We both were, I mean, we are, worried.

Well here I am. I say. Myself.

Exactly. He smiles at me. Let's enjoy the evening then. Will I order some wine?

We sink into the night and I am trying to be in it with him.

Any ladies on the scene Esther?

No Dad.

Men?

No Dad.

You should think about getting a dog, he says. A dog would be great company for you.

My landlord won't even let me put posters up.

A small one, he says. No trouble, the small ones.

Plus I can't afford a dog.

They don't eat much, the small ones.

Okay Dad.

Listen, I should head to my train. It was great to see you, love. Your mother was asking for you. Send her a text, would you.

A text saying what?

Anything. Just tell her something, she'd love to hear from you.

Okay. I will.

Good girl.

Pause.

Dad –

Yeah?

Casual, like it's a throwaway question.

There was something I wanted to ask you, actually, before you go.

Go on then.

If you were to describe me in one word, what would that word be?

What a funny question.

Humour me.

Pause.

Smart, he says. You've always been clever. All those good marks. It's a gift, that. You can do anything you put your mind to. Absolutely anything. Don't forget it.

Thanks, Dad.

Enjoy it, he says. That's your ration of compliments for the year.

***

Smart.

It's Friday and I'm standing in an open-plan office warehouse conversion.

Robert Decking, CEO, is sitting on an orange beanbag. He pats an adjacent beanbag in teal.

You must be Esther.

Hello, I say, it's lovely to meet you.

You know who I am.

Yes, I say, I wasn't expecting, I thought I'd be meeting a HR person –

That's not how we do things here, Esther. We've got a more personal approach.

He smiles a wide canyon smile.

I sit. I try to cross my legs, then remember I'm wearing a skirt. I hug my knees, then feel like a toddler. I settle for bending them to one side and await the ensuing pins and needles.

Welcome, he says, to the home of innovation and disruption!

I gaze over his shoulder at his Nespresso machine.

Thanks.

I just thought we'd have a chat. Get to know each other a little better.

Okay, I say.

I just want to ask you a few quick things.

Go ahead.

I've read your CV and I'm a big fan, so you can relax!
I suppose I'm just, well if I'm honest, it was the strangest thing, because you've got all this experience, you know project-management experience out the wazoo, for your age Esther it's really impressive – but I'm reading and it strikes me that I'm not sure I can see *you* in it, you know, who *you* are.

Oh. I say.

Because we're looking for individuals here. Singular minds. Dynamic trailblazers. You know? And so I wonder if, first of all, if you could tell me who Esther Nutting *really* is. Let's start with this one – what you think your greatest strength is? Forgive me the ol' tried-and-tested question, ha ha, but I think it's a great one.

Smart.

What's that? he says.

I'm smart. I think I can do anything I put my mind to.

Pause.

He grins me his piano-key fillings.

I like that you're owning it, Esther, that's what we like to see here, we're after that kind of balls-to-the-wall confidence, if you'll forgive the phrase in the presence of a lady!

He chuckles. I do a polite smile and hate myself.

And here's the second question – what about your greatest weakness?

I think back to the list, I read it this morning I –

I'm a perfectionist. A militant perfectionist.

He shifts his weight. The beans crash around like the sea.

Is that right? And why do you think that's a weakness?

I'm opening my mouth before I've had a chance to think.

Because I'm never satisfied, I run myself ragged, I can't stop until everything is perfect and not just perfect according to me but objectively, actually perfect. Like you know there are structures in the world that say who's the best and who is just average and I want whatever I do to be the best by every metric, even new metrics that still haven't been invented. I want everything I do to be the best. I need it to be. Otherwise, I don't see the point in doing anything.

I can hear myself slowly veering off the rails but I keep speaking I can't stop it coming out –

Otherwise if I thought that wasn't achievable I'd do nothing.
But the mad bit is I don't even want it to be achievable.
I want it to be so difficult that it seems impossible. And then
I want to be the one to do it.

Silence.

Then Robert Decking, CEO, mimes falling off his beanbag.

Well, he says, I'm floored.

He holds out his hand, beaming.

Welcome to the company, Esther.

Do you have any questions?

I look at his hand, meaty outstretched.

Pause.

Am I real?

Pause.

No. I don't say that.

I stand up on legs full of fizzing static. That's when I run.

***

It got tricky, with her, to remember where I stopped and she
started. I'd sometimes forgot whose limbs were whose,
waking up sleepy to scratch my leg and she'd ask what I was
doing and could I please cut my nails. Joked once about
wanting to find a zip in her skin, climb into it and wear it
over my own.

Can't work out if that's sweet, or a bit *Silence of the Lambs.*

Imagine. It'd be like one of those rain ponchos you get at
festivals.

You're such a freak, Es.

Now you know.

I already knew.

She runs a finger down my spine.

Come here you.

***

In the mornings, before I get out of bed I reach for my notepad. I read the list out loud like a recipe.

Perfectionist. Smart. No-Nonsense. Feet Firmly On The Ground.

Maura's turning thirty-three and hosting what she's insisting on calling an 'intimate gathering'. Sounds like an *Eyes Wide Shut* party, I told her, and I refuse to attend a sex party with an immediate family member. But here I am anyway, late and bleeding from both knees.

What happened to you?!

Fell up the hill.

I'll find you a plaster.

You're wearing it!

The cloth brooch I made her is splashed on her chest, gold silk against the black dress she looks so good in but rarely wears.

Course I am, it's beautiful. You could sell these, I'm telling you.

I just smile.

I'm serious! Derek could help you with the marketing, get a website set up, all that. Couldn't you, babe?

He's stood at her shoulder eating a nacho like an awkward sentinel.

Yeah, I mean that's all pretty entry-level stuff, but I'd be happy to.

You should really think about it, Maura pushes. You could make real money from them.

I don't want to sell them. That's not the point.

What is the point then?

She's genuinely confused.

They're just for fun.

Fun! She laughs.

That's your youth talking. I don't have time to do anything fun any more.

Wordlessly, Derek hands her a margarita.

I'm just at a stage in my life when I need to focus on my career before it's too late, you know, and –

Derek puts on some nondescript electronica and starts sort of nodding to it, like he's politely agreeing with himself.

There just only is so much time, Es, as a woman, to really *establish* yourself, to, I suppose really *leave your mark* –

Babe? Derek says.

Yeah babe?

That was the doorbell.

Well can't you get it?

I'm not sure who it is.

Well yes babe that is the function of a door in that it obscures the identity of the person on the other side of the door.

You get it, he says, I'll keep Essie company.

I'm fine, I say, I'm

Alright, she says, I'm going, I'm going. Try to at least pretend to enjoy yourself, you two.

She flounces off.

Can I get you a drink, Essie? Derek says.

Got one thanks. I indicate the cup I'm holding.

Oh, course you have. How are you, anyway?

Fine, I say.

Good, that is very good. How's the job hunt going?

Fine. Fine.

You'll find something. I know you will. Maura tells me you're very driven, a real self-starter.

Does she.

That's what you need to have in this economy, real get-up-and-go, you know, I mean certainly I know from my experience that building websites is an oversaturated market, you know, and so I've really had to stamp on a few heads along the way. You know. Crush a few skulls.

Pause.

He raises his empty wine glass to his lips and takes a sip of air.

Listen, we should go for a coffee.

A coffee?

His tone is light and breezy, like this is a perfectly normal occurrence, like we often spend time just the two of us when in fact the last time was at Maura's summer barbecue when she had to nip to the shop for ice and Derek and I spent an excruciating twenty minutes trying to introduce people we did not know to each other.

Yeah. He says. Maybe on Saturday? I'd love to give you a hand setting up that website.

Maura must have told him to make more effort to get to know me. That's exactly the sort of thing she'd do.

Oh. Oh that's – nice of you, but I've actually got plans on Saturday, I say.

Right. He says. No problem.

Some other time, maybe.

Yeah. Course.

Maura comes back into the room trailed by two devastatingly beautiful women. I swear that girl cuts her friends out of *Vogue*.

She puts one arm around each of us.

How are my favourite wallflowers doing?

I think Derek's flirting with me, I say.

Please, she says, don't let me stand in the way of love.

Derek looks at his glass. I need a top-up.

Be right back, Maura says, as the door pings again. I'll bring you that plaster.

Blood's running into my socks.

***

When I wake in the mornings, the body in my bed is like a stranger. I look down at it and tell myself I am lying in it. A shadow in clear water.

Perfectionist. Smart. No-Nonsense. A Self-Starter. Feet Firmly On The Ground.

A friend from my old job says I'm bubbly. I picture bits of me rising into my head and evaporating through my scalp.

You were the life and soul of the office! Friday-night drinks just aren't the same without you!

When I ask for tap water he pours some of his sparkling into my glass without saying anything. I can put in a good word with Rachel, he says, if you'd want to come back.

No thank you.

I don't really know why you left in the first place if I'm honest, Esther, he says.

They let me go, actually.

His face sags. It's funny to watch. I watch myself in my chair watching his face.

I had heard that, but I didn't believe it. Why, if you don't mind me asking?

Because well I sort of gradually started to notice that I was stones. Sludgy silt gathering first on my tongue. Grit in my teeth. Spit black in the sink at night. Went to the dentist and she said it was plaque. But then the pebbles start forming, small and wave-washed smooth and the piles they make have spaces in between where the edges don't slot together and I start to rattle slightly when I walk. And at first I just put my clothes over my skin and my coat over my clothes and left the house like nothing was wrong like I wasn't actually a skin-bag full of stones. On the bus, excuse me, just a normal human person coming through, nothing to see here. Nothing to see here.

But the stones kept piling up higher. My clothes started to bulge in weird places as my skin rippled and dimpled and I stopped letting anyone touch me. Turned handshakes into waves. When they got to my chest it got difficult to get up in the morning. I mean that literally, I wanted to get up and get out the door but a large quantity of small stones really weighs a surprising amount and it was an enormous effort even to sit up. And so I started to stay in bed and when I did manage to haul myself in to the office the stones sort of sat behind my eyes in a passive-aggressive pile and made everything a bit grey round the edges and that made it quite difficult to see my screen, or listen in meetings or really just get any work done.

And that's when I stopped coming to work and when I'd used up all my sick days and then some, they had to very gently, very tactfully, let me go. We love you Essie, they said, and if you love someone, you let them go.

I say, contract was up and they decided not to renew it. Probably so they didn't have to increase my salary, the bastards.

Cheapskates. I hope you're keeping busy?

As a bee.

Fun fact, he says, bees are not actually that busy. A recent study in a Chinese province that replaced bees with people found conclusively Esther, it found absolutely conclusively that a person can pollinate flowers at a considerably quicker rate than a bee can. People don't waste time faffing around between each flower, you see. They just get on with it.

He pushes his glasses up his nose.

What a time to be alive.

Isn't it.

It's good, he says, that you're busy. It's very important to keep busy. It can't be easy, sitting around doing nothing.

It's temporary.

You know, the office was subsidising these mindfulness classes for us, I found them very useful to stay focused, you know, keep my productivity up. I've got an app for it on my phone now and everything. Though Andy and Helen upped and quit after they'd done the six classes. They packed it all in and decided to open a sheep farm in Dorset. Rachel cancelled the classes after that, bit of a shame.

I suppose you can be too mindful, can't you.

Exactly, he says gravely.

Have you thought about giving it a try? Meditation?

They'd love that wouldn't they, to get us all to be calm and compliant, that's their corporate wet dream. Billions of people sitting nice and quietly trying to make their minds go blank. I only feel whole when I'm angry, and even then, only for a second.

I'll look in to it, I say.

On the bus home I add the word to the list. Bubbly.

***

Perfectionist. Smart. Bubbly. A Self-Starter. No-Nonsense. Feet Firmly On The Ground.

Perfectionist. Smart. Bubbly. A Self-Starter. No-Nonsense. Feet Firmly On –

I thought we needed to have a bit of a chat.

Liz has brought me out for lunch. She's insisted on paying. I'm really focused on my steak, sharp knife gliding through the rare flesh.

Essie?

Mm. Yeah. I say.

I'm worried about you.

Chew. Oh?

I've watched you mope around for months now, and I think you need to start changing your outlook. Invest in yourself. You'd be surprised how much it might help.

I put down my steak knife.

You need to think about what you want, Essie. What do *you
really want?*

What do you mean?

I mean in life!

Swallow.

I don't know.

I mean, where do you want to be?

Pause.

Where do you see yourself?

Pause.

I want to be tiny.

Pause.

You can do anything you want.

Pause.

I want to be nowhere.

Pause.

But you need to start making some plans. Like, what you're
going to do when your savings run out. Have you thought
about that at all?

Yeah –

And? What are you going to do, Es?

Get a job. Any job. Do that job until I'm eighty. Then die
I guess?

I'm trying to quip but she's stony-faced.

Oh here we go.

She puts down her fork.

What?

Nothing, she says. Trying to button it back in but it's spilling
out all over her face.

If you've got something to say to me, just say it.

Alright then. I will. I want you to grow the fuck up.

Pause.

Grow up and get over yourself. We're not nineteen any more, Es and I've had just about enough.

Is that right, I say, soft.

You think you're so much better than everyone else, than me and the rest of us with our steady jobs and our pension plans, you think you're *above* all of that. You always have. You think we're all sheep and you're some kind of miraculous fucking giraffe stood in the middle looking down on us.

I –

You think I haven't noticed you sneering at me every time I tell a story about my work, because I actually enjoy my job and get on with my colleagues, heaven forbid! And yeah, what I do isn't rocket science. It's not brain surgery. But do you know what, I count myself lucky to have a job that lets me have a nice life and at least I'm contributing something to the world instead of sat on my ass all day every day.

I try to speak, and falter.

You know you haven't asked me once about me or how I am in the last six months? Not once.

I.

Pause.

That's not true.

Silence.

Well go on then, how are you?

She's quivering.

I'm not great, as it happens. Hayley dumped me while we were on holiday, right in the middle of the holiday so that was pretty shit.

Her arms are folded tight like she's holding her heart in.

I scrabble around in the air.

I don't know what to say – I've been, well it's just –

What?

I don't know if what I say is real. If anything I do, is real. It's like one day I woke up and noticed that everything's hollow and now I can't unsee it, I can't go back. Every gesture is empty, like – a bowl full of air.

Like, if I do something nice, I worry that what other people might observe in me as a consideration for people's feelings, as kindness, is completely wrapped up in my own desire for people to see me as kind, as considerate. I'm afraid that everything I have ever done for someone else has been about me. About trying to control the way I am viewed in the world. I'm forever saying sorry and it looks like a haste to make sure that I haven't caused offence – that's good, right? That's decent. Wrong. What I'm doing, what I'm doing really is checking that my own image is still intact in the mind of the other person. Even this thought has originated from the worry that other people may think I am using them as a kind of mirror. Even this thought is about me.

I'll tell you what I really want. I want to jump out of my brain and into a kind of glass vessel where I can see everything impartially. Imagine that? I can't. No one can.

It's just what, Essie?

It's just – well that is shit, about Hayley.

Yeah. She says.

But.

What?

Don't you think there are lots of things that are so much worse?

Pause.

People are sleeping on the streets, people are drowning off the coast of Greece or beaten up by their spouses or by the police or get cancer at thirty or twenty or ten. People work every hour they're sent and still can't feed their families.

Pause.

So really Liz you're lucky. You're fucking lucky, actually. Don't you ever think about how fucking lucky you are?

Pause.

She starts to cry, almost completely silently, tears streaming down her face. She waves for the waiter. She pays for both our meals. She leaves a fifteen per cent tip. She takes a tissue from her bag and dabs her face, checks her make-up.

She looks at me.

She goes.

***

I thought Sandy, for the right one.

Sandy? She says.

It suits. Don't you think it suits?

Sounds like a dog's name.

What about Sandy from *Grease*?

You want to name my right knee after Sandy from *Grease*?

It's got that vibe. Like it might at any moment come of age and start to dress in leather.

Does it, she says.

Trust me. And for the left one – Brendan.

Brendan?

Brendan. Fucking – Brendan?

You promised. You promised I could name them anything I wanted.

And this is what you've chosen.

It's a good dependable name, Brendan. Can't go wrong.

I think we've already gone wrong, she says, I think something went wrong around the time you requested to name my knees?

Elbows next week, I say. I thought, maybe Stiletto, and Bread?

What, she says, laughing.

The only two types of knives I know.

Listen can I take you back to the shop? She says. Any chance of a full refund?

Fuck off.

As if, she says. Sure what would you do without me.

***

Perfectionist. Smart.

Monday morning. Suit jacket.

Bubbly. A Self-Starter.

Hair brushed. Collar as stiff as my resolve.

No-Nonsense. Feet Firmly On The Ground.

So Esther.

I'm holding the interviewer's gaze and thinking bizarrely in this most formal of moments about kissing her. What if I just kissed her.

She's holding my CV.

I can see here that you've been out of work for a little while, is that right?

I nod. Her voice is kind.

That must be tough.

I nod again.

Can you tell me what you've been doing with your time?

Well, I say. I've been job-hunting.

Of course. Of course you have. Job-hunting can really feel like a full-time job, can't it?

If only it paid.

She laughs uneasily.

But what else have you been up to, in your free time? Volunteering – learning a language – or a new skill? Could you tell me a little bit about what you've been up to?

Oh.

I remember what Maura told me. Just be yourself.

Well.

Take your time, she says.

Well, I walk. I go for walks.

Oh?

She's sitting up. Well that's excellent, she says, Marie on our HR team does charity walks regularly, she's raised over seven thousand pounds for breast-cancer research.

Be myself. Be myself. I need her to know the truth.

Not for charity, I say.

Well that doesn't matter, I mean, hiking in nature can be so beautiful, can't it. So uplifting.

I need someone to know the whole truth about me.

I walk around the city. At night, mostly. Just to walk.

I need someone to know the whole truth about me and say, that's okay. You are okay.

Pause.

She pulls back.

Right, she says, still so kindly, achingly kind.

Thank you so much for coming in, Esther. We'll be in touch.

***

I'm looking at some exposed brick thinking I know how it feels. The list is clamped in my sweaty hand, paper worn thin and shiny now.

Essie? Caroline calls to me from a table for two. She is wearing a new coat, snug and glossy and I'm so thrown by it that when I sit down I open my mouth to say hello and what comes out is

How's your coat

What, she says

Your coat. It's new.

Yeah.

Nice.

Thanks.

Yeah.

Pause.

Sorry I'm late, I walked past this place twice. What's with the medicine sign out front?

It's been converted from an old 1960s pharmacy.

But how are people supposed to know it's a café?

I dunno, she says. I guess they just sense it?

She raises an eyebrow at me and I crack a smile. Then stop. Remember.

So.

It's nice to see you, she says.

Is it?

Yeah.

Pause.

How have you been?

Yeah good I say.

Keeping busy?

As a bee.

I saved a bee's life the other day, she says. It was lying on my doorstep on its back, sort of, flailing. I read somewhere to give it a spoonful of sugar and water and it perked right up. I'd had a long day and I thought about just walking right past it but then I thought, look at this poor defenceless creature. I have a duty towards this creature as a citizen of the earth.

Not defenceless, I say. Famously.

She sips her coffee.

Pause.

I planned this so well but now that I am here and she is sitting across from me close enough to touch, my question seems impossible.

Pause.

Bubbly.

What? she says.

I – Well I'm making a list of words that describe me and I wondered if you had any to add.

My hand trembles as I take it out of my pocket and show her.

It's for interviews. It's just for my job interviews.

She takes it.

Pause.

What is this?

I told you, I say, it's a list of words that describe me.

Pause.

This could be anyone, Essie.

At the table opposite it is a child's birthday and he is crying because the helium balloon tied around his finger is too tight. His mother is trying to unpick the knot.

She's reading it again.

There's so many words on here, Caroline says, it could describe absolutely anyone.

Pause.

Can you give it back? I say, casual.

Why are you doing this?

The boy's finger is free. The balloon floats up to the rafters, clings to the roof. He studies the sharp red welt the string has left.

I find it helpful. It's just something to refer to, is all –

This worries me.

Pause.

I still care about you.

Well you should stop, I say. Caring.

I'd love to Essie, I really would love to but it's not that easy.

Seemed pretty easy before.

The waitress comes and asks if we are finished with our tiny coffees. We nod and she takes away the cups and now we have not even the posture of drinking coffees, now we are just two people having a hard and intense conversation in a refurbished pharmacy.

Pause.

Do you really want to talk about this. She says.

Don't you?

No.

Why did you show up then?

I came here today to tell you that I've forgiven you.

Oh. I say.

I've forgiven you and I want you to be happy. I think given the circumstances, that is more than you should reasonably expect.

Can I have it back, I say again. The list.

That is more than you should reasonably expect given that you seem to have forgotten that you smashed up our living room.

Pause.

You seem to have forgotten that you threw a plate at my head.

Pause.

Have you. Forgotten. She says.

Pause.

Something lifted and you saw me under it. Maggots under a stone.

GIVE IT BACK.

I mean to just say it but I shout it. People turn around in their chairs to stare at us. Caroline puts the list down on the table.

I heard about this service, recently, she says. Called a Rage Room.

She's putting on her new coat that's a little too tight under the arms.

You pay by the hour to hire a room to go and smash stuff with a baseball bat. Padded walls, you can scream as much as you like.

I start to put on my coat and we're in a race now, who can get it on quicker, who can leave the other sitting alone at this table, my coat is old and well-worn which is giving me a competitive edge.

It allows people to work through their rage in a healthy way, so it doesn't, you know, spill out. Spill over into their work lives. Their relationships.

She's turning for the door, her shiny trenchcoat halfway to her shoulders like a crumpled person trying to hitch a ride on her back.

Maybe give it a try, she says.

She turns to go.

Caroline.

Yes, she says, soft.

Am I real?

Pause.

No. I don't say that.

She looks at me.

Take care.

***

Home in a blur. Pass ticket barrier train door stand hand hold the rail train door ticket barrier front door to bedroom door. Shut it.

Press my back against the closed door. Slide down it onto the floor like they do in soaps. Did that go from life to telly or from telly to life. Is it real.

Take out the list and start to read.

ESTHER

Perfectionist

Smart

Bubbly

A Self-Starter

No-Nonsense

Feet Firmly On The Ground.

Text my mum Mum what am I like. She says I'm personable, tell them you're personable that's a good word she says people like people who are personable she says. Thanks I say, and she replies saying something else but I don't reply instead I email an old school friend. Shy, she says, I always thought you were a bit shy, if I'm honest, sorry what's this for again? Ring my primary-school principal. Outgoing, he says, you'd chat to anyone, I remember, nice to hear from you Call an old boss. A team player he says, if you ever need a reference I'd be happy to

ESTHER

Perfectionist

Smart

Bubbly

A Self-Starter

No-Nonsense

Feet Firmly On The Ground

Personable

Outgoing

Chatty

Shy

A team player.

I read it again.

ESTHER

Perfectionist

Smart

Bubbly

A Self-Starter

No-Nonsense

Feet Firmly On The Ground

Personable

Outgoing

Chatty

Shy

A team player.

Again. Again. Again. Again. Again.

***

I shorten my commute. Bedroom to kitchen to living room to kitchen to bedroom. I build a tiny kingdom and watch my savings dribble away like the weeks. I am not a recluse. I have to eat. I become a tide, inching out to the corner shop, ebbing back with floating jetsam, crisps and milk and beans.

I spend a lot of time on the internet. The internet knows me so well. The internet tells me which cute animal I am (lamb). Which John Hughes movie I am (*Pretty in Pink*). Which classic car I am (Cadillac). Which roasted meat I am (lamb). Which sandwich I am (BLT). Which major European city I am (Paris). Which condiment I am (Mustard). Which type of shoe I am (kitten heel). Which element I am on the Periodic Table (Neon). Which type of rabbit I am (dwarf). Which US President I am (Nixon. Nixon? I try again.

Obama). The internet tells me that I'm an introvert. The
internet tells me I'm an extrovert. The internet tells me
I sometimes like to go out and sometimes to stay in.

The internet tells me I'm a Miranda, a Ravenclaw, a Mulan,
a Laura Palmer. A dog person, a winter person, a cupcake
person, a summer person, a martini person, a bird person.
A beach person, a city person, a forest person, a cat person,
a lake person, a boat person.

The internet tells me that I am a person and that is.

I want to hold on to that.

I sit in my room and read the news, watch the news, live-
stream the news. If I could I'd pay monthly for an
intravenous drip of news. Maybe if it went straight into my
blood I would feel it.

All of the carnage the dead children the drowned parents the
families fleeing wholesale on the back of a truck only to fall
into traffic at a border just waiting to turn them away. The
floods and storms and hurricanes, the planet bucking like a
horse trying to throw us all off and out into space, trying to
warn us to stop what we're doing but we keep doing it, we do
it more and more and more and more and this morning Steven
Bradley fifty-seven found dead next to a pile of freshly printed
CVs his benefits had recently been cut the tusks off and sell
them on the black market the white rhino has become
officially extinct with the death of the last female in existence
and hi @skycustomerservice my modem still has not arrived
missing since Tuesday please share his family want him home
safe and sound Friday's here and we're giving away a
weekend for two in the telephone lines have been cut in Puerto
Rico and our daughter has lost contact with us can you PayPal
here to help to help to help by donating to our Kickstarter our
GoFundMe you can be part of something that matters.

I sit in my room and click on the next and the next and the
next tragedy. I sit in my room helpless and numb and I do
absolutely nothing.

I watch videos of soldiers coming home for Christmas, their
kids running into their arms I watch videos of people seeing
their grandkids for the first time on Skype I

watch videos of people singing people crying people fighting people ranting people fucking I

watch videos of hedgehogs being washed cats falling asleep ducklings learning to swim dogs playing pianos children playing with dogs I

watch videos of people doing their make-up doing their weekly shop doing their taxes doing their best in front of the judges and then I find myself back watching Mary tell the doctor she feels she is a normal person, at least her husband certainly thinks so and then the LSD goes down the hatch and the way her face slowly changes like dawn across a kitchen floor and that one that one that one moment when the doctor says 'Mary, how do you feel?'

And she smiles that serene smile.

'Why, doctor, there is no me. There is no you.'

I play the video again. There is no me. And again. There is no you. And again. And again. And again. And again. And again. And again until I drift off into the inky dark and when I wake I'm not sure what time it is.

I reach for the list. But it's nowhere to be found.

I look in my pockets my bags my bed my floor my drawers my pillowcase and it is not anywhere.

I look again.

I look again and I am not anywhere not on the ceiling not under the bed not in the cracks between the floorboards not in the teastains on my constellation of dirty mugs not in the dust in the corners not in a dirty sock or the wastepaper bin.

I am not in the creases of my dresses hanging I am not in the laundry basket or on top of the wardrobe not in the hem of the curtains not in the light seeping under the door –

I am not

in the hardwearing carpet on the stairs or under the rug in the hall or in the tissue in the right sleeve of my coat or in the bolt of my front door or the slam that claps the air as I hurl myself onto the street into a small crowd of tourists doing a prepaid organised tour of the most famous examples of anti-establishment graffiti in this area I am

I am nowhere. I am

ESSIE *starts to say some of the words of the list in a jumble.*

Personable. Chatty. Militant perfectionist. Bubbly, self-starter team player. Shy militant perfection-ist, bubbly, self-starter outgoing. Militant perfection-ist blovely, self-smarter, militant perfect, catty sly person able, outgoing, personable, person able out going out going out out out

***

It's late and the train carriage is a gallery of tired faces.

Not me not me not me not me not me not me.

Not me not me not me not me not me not me.

Everyone's quiet on this train. Everyone except a young man sitting next to me who's talking loudly on the phone.

It's a disgrace what they're doing to me, he's saying, a disgrace.

Everyone is holding themselves back in their seats and very intently not looking at him. A kind of anti-energy, this not-looking.

It's sabotage, yeah? Full-on sabotage, they think I can't see that, and when I went down there they wouldn't see me without an appointment! I'm at the end of my – I have a degree I told them that, I've got a degree, I've got a lot to OFFER do you know what I'm saying?

I suddenly realise that we've been underground for five minutes now.

And they told me, they told me yeah that it wasn't real. That my SYMPTOMS yeah, all the tests yeah, they did TESTS and they found NOTHING! And I said, well look again mate! You'll find it if you LOOK AGAIN!

I listen to the phone he's pressed to his right ear inches from my left ear. There's no one on the other end of the line.

We reach a stop and loads of people get off.

Practical. No-Nonsense. Self-Starter.

Yeah yeah that's what I told them he says I told them that I did but they didn't listen, I didn't shout no I said it real soft. I said it real soft.

The carriage is silent, the train moving off again.

I really tried to be real soft and gentle with them and not shout you know – but I'll get them, they don't know who they're dealing with. How powerful I am. They've got no idea who I am.

Personable. Feet firmly on the ground. Feet firmly on the

No idea what kind of force they're messing with, do you know what I'm saying, what kind of man I am? Cos I am powerful, he says, so loud that people look up from their *Metro*s and *Standard*s.

He turns to me.

I AM POWERFUL, he shouts.

Someone shh-es him.

Oh yeah? He beats his chest.

You can't stop me because me yeah me, I AM FUCKING POWERFUL!

I am the only one looking at him. He stares right back at me.

Then he stands up and slips out the doors into the pouring crowd.

I look resolutely at the filthy ground. I am not that man, I tell myself. I am not the woman stood opposite me, hands in her pockets, I am not her pockets. I am not the railing, I am not this seat. I am, I am. Perfectionist. Bubbly. Shy self-starter outgoing. Confident. Personable. Smart. I look at the hands in my lap and tell myself they're my hands, my hands. My hands curled tight in hers, my hands curled tight in fists my hands my hand my. Pinch my arm. Smart. Smart.

At 4 a.m., I find myself at my own front door. And I'm not the only one.

***

Another actor enters. It's DEREK. ESSIE *and* DEREK *look at one another.*

ESSIE. What the fuck are you doing here?

DEREK. Can I come in?

ESSIE. Is – Maura with you?

DEREK. No. She doesn't know I'm here, actually.

ESSIE. Is she okay?

DEREK. Oh yes. Fine. She's making dal.

ESSIE. What?

DEREK. Dal, she's making a big batch of. Look. Is this a – really bad time, or –

ESSIE. Come in. Be my guest.

They go into ESSIE'*s kitchen. Suddenly made real.*

DEREK. Well.

ESSIE. Well.

Pause.

It's late, Derek. What's up?

DEREK. I arrived at about ten.

ESSIE. So you've just been sat on my step?

DEREK. Mmm.

ESSIE. Why?

DEREK. I'll explain.

Long silence.

Your birthday's next week.

ESSIE. Yeah?

DEREK. We should do something. With Maura I mean we should all. Go out.

ESSIE. Is that what you came all this way to tell me?

DEREK. No.

ESSIE. What then?

Pause.

DEREK. You. You look.

ESSIE. What?

DEREK. Tired. Really tired.

ESSIE. Thanks mate.

An even longer silence.

Can you spit it out? Whatever it is?

DEREK. I don't. Eh I don't really know the words for it. You know.

ESSIE. No. I haven't a clue. I need words.

DEREK. Course, course.

Pause.

I've been thinking.

He shifts from foot to foot.

Well, it was what you said – the thing you said the other day that got me thinking.

ESSIE. The other day?

DEREK. When Maura and I took you for dinner.

ESSIE. Three months ago.

DEREK. Was that three months ago? Jesus. The weeks.

ESSIE. Yeah.

DEREK. Well – I've been trying to talk to you since then. Been meaning to, and I suppose I've come here because I've not been able to get it out of my head and I wanted to, eh – just to say that, well I, I sort of know what you mean about all that stuff you were saying.

ESSIE. What stuff?

DEREK. About the – chair. You said you felt like – and I well.
I mean I sometimes, well I've actually, often enough. Felt
like that. What I mean is, I actually, feel like that – all the
time Essie. All the – well all the fucking time.

Pause.

And I think – well I came here to say – to tell you – I really
think it'll be alright. You'll be. I mean, I dunno do I, what do
I know about any of this stuff, but for what it's worth – I think
that it might be – it might all be alright.

Long pause.

ESSIE. Christ. You should be a motivational speaker.

DEREK. Oh piss off.

ESSIE. Derek?

DEREK. Yeah?

ESSIE. Am I real?

Pause.

DEREK. Yes.

Pause.

ESSIE. Okay.

DEREK. Okay?

ESSIE. Okay.

ESSIE *reaches out to* DEREK. *Touches him.*

Okay?

DEREK. Okay.

End of play.

INSIDE VOICES

Nabilah Said

NABILAH SAID

Nabilah Said is a playwright, arts reviewer and poet whose plays have been presented in Singapore and London. She has written eight plays to date, including *ANGKAT*, a festival commission of the M1 Singapore Fringe Festival 2019, and a reading of *yesterday it rained salt* at London's Bunker Theatre in 2017. In 2018, she founded Lazy Native, a theatre collective that champions Southeast Asian narratives in theatre. Nabilah is a former arts correspondent with English-language broadsheet *The Straits Times* and currently contributes reviews and features to *ArtsEquator* and *Exeunt Magazine*. Her short stories and poetry have been published by multiple Singapore publishers. She holds an MA in Writing for Performance at Goldsmiths, University of London. nabilahsaid.com

This version of *Inside Voices* was presented by Lazy Native and first performed at VAULT Festival, London, on 23 January 2019, with the following all-female and all-Asian cast and creative team.

NISA	Suhaili Safari
LILY	Siti Zuraida
FATIMAH	Nur Khairiyah Ramli
Director	Zhui Ning Chang
Producers	Deanna Dzulkifli
	Nur Khairiyah Ramli
Stage Manager	Muslihah Mujtaba
Sound Designer	Nicola Chang
Lighting Designer	Raycher Phua

Thank you to my teachers and friends from Goldsmiths; Lora and Rach from Global Voices Theatre; Gill Greer and the VAULT Festival team; Singapore's National Arts Council; and Tommo Fowler for their support and assistance with the development of this work. This play would not have been possible without the unending support of my family and friends from Singapore and all over the world. To Erfendi Dhahlan, thank you for always loving and believing, and for making space for your wife's anger at the world. This work is dedicated to the women of the Nusantara.

N.S.

Characters

NISA, *a married woman in her early twenties*
LILY, *an unmarried woman in her late thirties*
FATIMAH, *a married woman in her mid-fifties*

Note on Text

The characters sometimes use Arabic, Malay and Singlish (Singapore-English) words. Footnotes are provided for context only – surtitles are not necessary for a production.

Portions starting and ending with *** are meant to be delivered in a snappy, almost-rehearsed fashion.

ACT ONE

*What can be seen: A room, furnished just enough to
approximate someone's idea of a cosy communal space. There
should be a chest or box that contains all the named props and
costumes.*

*Three women, NISA, LILY and FATIMAH, are standing in the
middle of the space. They do not notice one another.*

Spotlights on each of them to reveal the following:

NISA *is stirring two cups of coffee. She sits down and sips from
her cup. The other cup is untouched.*

FATIMAH *is cleaning a table. Every time she is done, she
starts wiping it again. She does not sit.*

LILY *is trying on a silk hijab[1] as she watches a video on her
phone. She is not doing a very good job. She removes the hijab.*

Upbeat music plays. The women are jolted into action.

LILY (*stretching*). Oof! (*Notices the other two women.*) Oh.
    You guys again.

NISA. Yes, who else were you expecting?

    LILY *doesn't respond. She massages the side of her neck.*

    What's wrong with your neck?

FATIMAH. Pain?

LILY. Financial year-end. You know.

NISA. Ah. (*Holds up her middle finger.*) Me too.

    FATIMAH *gives* NISA *a look.* NISA *retracts her finger,
    while suppressing a giggle.* LILY *looks triumphant, but she
    laughs too.*

FATIMAH (*to* NISA). Neese. The food, takeout please.

NISA. Yes, *Kak.*[2]

---

1. Veil.
2. Sister. *Kak* is a shortform for *Kakak.*

FATIMAH. Don't call me *Kakak* lah. I'm not so old, you know.

NISA *fetches food and puts it on the table*. FATIMAH *inspects the food*.

Eh, you all, yesterday I dream again.

NISA. The Zumba class one?

FATIMAH. Yah. The instructor she ask me to take over the class... she say she want to go toilet or what. Some nonsense reason. But I cannot remember all the things she teach. So I think lah about what I know. (*Does the moves which resemble the action she describes, using her entire body.*) Like, okay... sweep sweep sweep the floor. Wipe wipe wipe window. Stir the curry, stir the curry, stir the curry so it doesn't stick! Terrible, you know.

LILY. Cool what. Sounds like a rap.

LILY *and* NISA *laugh*. FATIMAH *laughs too*.

NISA (*to* FATIMAH). I'm sorry, Kak.

FATIMAH. Don't be nonsense. No need to be sorry... Just a dream only.

LILY (*to* FATIMAH). What song was it? Zumba music always happening.

FATIMAH. Ah... (*Sings the song 'Work' by Rihanna, in an unrecognisable tune.*)

'Work work work work...' Something like that. Woman singer one.

NISA (*laughing*). That's Riri lah, Kak. Rihanna.

FATIMAH. I thought Malay. 'Rai-ha-nah' you know? I thought, what a good Malay girl, working so hard.

LILY *starts singing the song and dancing in an exaggerated sexy manner towards a reluctant* FATIMAH, *who waves her away*.

Beat.

The three women sit at the table and start to eat.

NISA (*chewing*). Mmm... This chicken. *Sedap!*[3]

---

3. Delicious.

LILY (*chewing*). Delicious.

FATIMAH (*chewing*). *Ketumbar?*[4] I can taste ketumbar.

LILY (*to* NISA). Eh, Neese, where's your rice?

NISA. Don't have.

LILY. What?

NISA. I'm on a no-carb diet.

LILY. Why?

NISA. Want to lose weight.

LILY. Why?

NISA. Why you so *kaypoh*?[5]

LILY. Relax lah, just asking only... Why, you yesterday never *get* any issit?

NISA. Don't be gross.

FATIMAH *shoots a warning look to* LILY.

FATIMAH (*to* NISA). You know it doesn't matter if we eat rice *ke*,[6] sandwich ke, banana split ke... Got no difference outside.

NISA (*to* FATIMAH). But Kak, what if I develop a... a taste for it. What if my body remembers later, and then I want more? (*Beat. To herself, mostly.*) No rice for me.

FATIMAH. Eh, cannot. Malay people cannot not eat rice.

LILY. It's the rice that soaks up all the gravy – that's the point of it. It isn't anything on its own. It needs all the other dishes to give it... personality. I mean... it's practically written in the How-To-Be-Asian handbook.

NISA (*to* LILY). I can taste the chicken just fine lah. (*To* FATIMAH.) Kak Mah, taste for me?

FATIMAH. Why, your tongue not working issit?

NISA. No lah. If you tell me what's inside, then I can try to figure out the recipe.

LILY. For what?

---

4. Coriander.
5. Nosy.
6. Or.

NISA. For my husband lah.

FATIMAH (*tasting*). Mm… Ketumbar… turmeric… sugar…

LILY (*to* NISA). What, fight again, issit?

NISA *does not reply.*

Beat.

Since when you like cooking?

NISA. I like cooking! I'm just… not good at it. He doesn't have flight this weekend and I want to cook – try to cook something for him. I need to put in more effort in the kitchen. I read that on a forum. To keep a man, women should spend some time in the kitchen, whipping up his favourite dishes. Whipping up. Why do they always say 'whipping up'?

LILY. 'Keep a man'? What is this, the nineties? Remind me to give you some new reading material. And says who women have to cook for men? Look at me – I Deliveroo everything. Simple.

FATIMAH. Lily, you don't understand. You don't have husband.

LILY (*mock-hurt*). Ouch Kak, brutal.

NISA. But you have to put effort. In a marriage. You have to put in the effort. Otherwise –

LILY. Otherwise he'll leave you for another woman?

NISA. Otherwise, you shouldn't be surprised if he… loses interest.

FATIMAH. Yah. Woman must look nice. If not, later look like a *nenek kebayan*.[7]

LILY *cackles like a witch.* NISA *prickles.*

NISA (*annoyed*). Don't do that!

LILY *laughs, normally this time.*

LILY (*to* FATIMAH). Kak, witches now hot lah. You never watch *Charmed*, issit? All three of them were so pretty. Sisters also.

---

7. Witch, presumably old and ugly.

NISA. The pretty ones are the worst.

FATIMAH. I don't know *Charmed*, I only know *Hocus Pocus*.

LILY. I rather be a witch than a good-for-nothing man. At least witches have power – even the ugly ones. Why should men get to have all the power? Why do we have to put in all this work, just for them?

NISA. It's not work.

FATIMAH. It's a responsibility. Husband must take care of wife. Wife must take care of husband.

LILY. I think women and men – humans – should just fuck when they want, leave and move on. No hard feelings.

NISA. Ugh.

FATIMAH. *Ish*.[8] Cannot like that.

LILY (*defiant*). Why cannot?

NISA. Cos then we'd be just like animals.

LILY. Well, are we that different? I mean, why do people even get married? Marriages break down. All the time. Shows you that something isn't right.

FATIMAH. Marriage is a blessing from God.

LILY. When it works.

FATIMAH (*frowns, realising*). Yes, marriage is also a test from God.

LILY. Exactly! A test! It requires way too much effort.

NISA. You're not making any sen– Let's just drop this, okay?

FATIMAH. Yes, don't waste time.

LILY. We just got here only. Can't we enjoy a bit?

FATIMAH (*gentle chiding*). You always want to enjoy. So, who this time?

LILY *starts to laugh*.

LILY. Oh my God. You guys are not going to believe it. So, I met this Chinese dude from Instagram right, who's a sergeant or whatever in the army. And he wanted me to call him – get this

8. Tsk.

okay – he wanted me to call him 'sir' while we were fucking.
Yah, seriously, like – (*Adopts a purposely obscene tone.*)
'Yes sir! Oh, yes, sir!'

FATIMAH *gives* LILY *a little slap on her thigh*.

NISA. No way!

LILY. Yah, like what the fuck right? I mean, the army and toxic
masculinity, how cliché! And, what, he thinks I'm serving
under him like one of his bitch-ass recruits issit? What a loser.

NISA. That's crazy. So, did you?

LILY. Hell no! (*Beat.*) I made him call me General.

NISA. No!

LILY. Yah. Turns out, he's *really* into the chain of command.

*There are high-fives – reluctant, indulging, incredulous. They
laugh, then recover.*

NISA. You don't use Tinder already?

LILY. Tinder is gross. Those guys just want sex.

NISA. But isn't that what –

LILY. There's wanting to have sex and there's *wanting* sex.
(*Seeing that* NISA *does not get it.*) Look.

LILY *takes out her phone and shows it to* NISA *and*
FATIMAH. *They both tilt their heads to see what is on
screen more clearly.*

NISA (*in recognition*). Is that a – !

NISA *squeals in disgust mixed with fascination.*

FATIMAH (*reacts one second later, in disgust, but also in
fascination*). Oh! (*Beat.*) God forgive me!

LILY. See? Desperation is gross. There has to be some mystery.

LILY *fetches glasses and a bottle of what looks like wine.
She inspects the bottle.*

Well, well.

LILY *uncaps the bottle and gives it a whiff. She tries to pour
the beverage into glasses.*

FATIMAH (*blocking her glass*). Eh –

LILY. It's just sparkling grape juice lah.

NISA. How you know?

LILY. Can't smell anything.

> LILY *continues pouring.* NISA *examines the bottle.*

Drink lah! Have as much as you want.

NISA. I shouldn't. It's all sugar.

> NISA *takes a sip, then she takes a bigger sip.* FATIMAH *observes her, then picks up her glass.*

FATIMAH. Just enjoy. We never get to enjoy.

> FATIMAH *drinks.*

LILY. Yes, finally. (*To* FATIMAH.) Kak, do the honours please.

FATIMAH (*holding up her glass*). To the three of us. Here together. Again.

LILY. To… suckling on the teat of this glorious life.

NISA. Ugh.

LILY. What? Okay okay. To… allowing ourselves to let go.

NISA (*sighs*). To not holding back. Not today.

LILY. Even with rice?

> FATIMAH *elbows* LILY *to shut up. The three women clink their glasses and drink.* LILY *downs her drink as if she is drinking a shot, slamming it on the table loudly.*

WHOO!

NISA. Shh!

FATIMAH. What?

> ***

NISA. The babies are sleeping.

LILY. Whose babies?

NISA. Ours.

FATIMAH. We have babies?

NISA. We could.

LILY. We might.

NISA. Some say we must.

FATIMAH. But we have?

NISA. Probably not.

FATIMAH. Okay.

    ***

    (*Beat*.) Rice?

LILY. We could, if we wanted to. Yes, please.

FATIMAH. What? Rice? Or children?

LILY. Both. The point is, it's our body and we have the right to
choose what we do with it. (*To* NISA.) Rice?

NISA. Oh, no. Thank you. (*To* FATIMAH.) My tummy a bit
weird. Can rub for me?

FATIMAH. Can.

LILY. What a baby.

FATIMAH (*to* LILY). Don't be like that.

    LILY *gives* NISA *a look*. FATIMAH *sits by* NISA *and rubs
    her tummy.*

NISA. Mmm… Just like Mama used to do. (*Beat*.) You know
people like to focus only on the miracle bit. Yes, sometimes
they talk about the blood, the screaming. The… (*Grimaces*.)
tearing. But then they skip past all that and suddenly you
supposed to magically love this – this thing you made. You
are expected to feel so much and forget the fact that you are
so changed. Forever changed.

    Lights flicker. FATIMAH *gestures for* NISA *to sit up and
    starts to massage her shoulders.*

It's like some sort of magic portal opens up. No one can see
it, except you. It swallows you. One half of you – goes.

Somewhere else. The other half has to carry on smiling and teaching and propping up and not giving up. (*Beat.*) I think I want some rice.

LILY. Good girl.

NISA *gets up and heads to the table.*

FATIMAH. Yes. Don't finish is a sin, you know.

FATIMAH *joins* LILY *and* NISA *at the table.*

LILY. My mother last time say, if you don't eat all of your rice, later the rice will cry. (*In an annoying baby voice, to* NISA.) Eat me, sis! Why you don't want me? Don't you love me? Wah wah wah!

NISA (*bothered*). *Diam*[9] lah.

They eat in silence for a few seconds.

LILY (*to* NISA*; gentle*). What happened?

NISA (*distracted*). Sometimes I can't – I have – I just want to close my eyes you know? And go away.

LILY. I know. I know. I'm sorry, okay?

LILY *strokes* NISA*'s hair.*

Beat.

NISA (*indicating the food*). There's still so much. Why do we have to finish it?

LILY. You know.

NISA. What?

LILY. You know.

NISA (*annoyed*). No, I don't know.

FATIMAH. For our sisters lah.

NISA. I don't have sisters.

LILY. Nonsense. We're all sisters.

LILY *starts to tie her hair up in a bun.*

We have to fight together. For all our fellow sisters.

---

9. Shut up.

NISA. But why?

FATIMAH *starts to put away the food*.

FATIMAH. No choice. We must do. For everyone.

NISA. But I don't care about the other women.

FATIMAH. What about us?

NISA. You two are different.

LILY. Are we that different? From all the other women who've come before? Chimamanda and Nawal El Saadawi and Khadijah –

FATIMAH (*interrupts*). Wife of the Prophet.

LILY *is slightly annoyed by the interruption*.

LILY. Yes –

FATIMAH (*interrupts*). Peace and blessings be upon Him.

LILY (*recovers*). Khadijah was a CEO of her time at a head of an empire. She was progressive and –

FATIMAH (*interrupts*). The mother of Islam.

LILY. Yes – We should be learning from all these women.

FATIMAH (*slightly pointed*). Yes, must learn.

LILY. Arm ourselves with knowledge.

FATIMAH. Religious knowledge –

LILY (*interrupts*). AND practical knowledge, of course. (*Beat.*) We have to look out for each other. Otherwise, no one else will.

LILY *helps* NISA *tie her hair*.

Beat.

Mak[10] asked me again, when am I going to get married.
I didn't know what to tell her. So I just said 'pray for me lah, Mak'. Ati says that Mak always asks her if I have a boyfriend. (*Laughs*.) I told Ati, tell her 'Ma'am is too busy to be dating right now.' Well, it's kinda true! I mean, Ati's salary isn't going to pay itself. She's worth it though. She's so strong, like man-strong. I don't know how she does it. Maybe it's in her

---

10. Mother.

blood – her family are farmers you know. Rice farmers. They have a rice field. Small one, but still. Living off the land. Isn't that amazing?

NISA *looks at* LILY *slightly askance.*

(*To* NISA.) Even a small amount of time to be ourselves should be cherished. Savoured. Kak Mah doesn't need to be in the kitchen. You don't need to feel guilty.

NISA. What about you?

LILY. I… I can be myself. (*More confidently.*) No, more than myself.

LILY *brushes a stray strand of hair from* NISA*'s face.*

Neese, we've been on the losing side for so long. It's our time now, but we have to use it wisely.

NISA *helps* FATIMAH *with her hair.*

NISA (*to* FATIMAH). Kak, teach me the recipe for the chicken, please?

FATIMAH. Okay –

LILY. No. We are not cooking. Not today.

NISA. But I want to do something productive.

LILY. The point of being here is not to recreate a domestic space.

NISA. Then why does it look like Kak Mah's living room?

FATIMAH. Eh, my living room cleaner. This one so messy, like a cat just gave birth.

They laugh.

NISA. I just want to learn –

FATIMAH. How to be good woman.

LILY. That's what people expect of us. We have to be good at work, good in bed, good in the kitchen… but no one can be fucking good all the time. I'm sorry, but it's exhausting. Why not be totally different?

LILY *retrieves a black niqab.*[11]

---

11. A veil that covers the head as well as the face, except for the eyes.

I tried this once. Just for fun. At first, we were all laughing, all my friends and me. But then I became all quiet. Inside I felt like shouting 'It's me! It's Lily! Can you see me?' But I didn't shout. I didn't say anything. (*Wears the niqab but does not cover her mouth.*) I left the store with a regular pink hijab. (*Beat.*) I don't even like pink.

LILY *retrieves two more niqabs and passes them to* NISA *and* FATIMAH.

NISA. That's why we're going with black?

LILY. Yes. Like witches. Isn't that perfect?

NISA. For what?

LILY. You know how men like to focus on how we look?

NISA. Yah?

LILY. Doesn't matter what we try to say. Once they see our external weaknesses, they point them out.

***

Like, my hair.

FATIMAH. My voice.

NISA. My body.

FATIMAH. My age.

LILY. My history.

NISA. My family.

***

LILY. We've seen it happen before, right? They shoot us down before they even give us a chance. I mean, just look at what happened to Malala. The old ways don't work any more. We have to innovate, sisters. They'll never attack us if we wear these. Not if we wear it like armour.

They nod at each other in an increasingly assured manner. NISA *and* FATIMAH *wear the niqab without covering their mouths.*

(*To* FATIMAH.) Ready Kak?

FATIMAH. Ready.

They stand in a row in silence for some moments. The mood is suspenseful.

Suddenly a jingle plays, indicating that they are in a cooking show like MasterChef. *The atmosphere becomes heightened. The tone is slightly hammy.*

NISA. So, Miss Fatimah, tell us, what's on the menu for us today?

FATIMAH. *Nasi Kangkang.*[12]

Gasps and claps from NISA *and* LILY.

LILY (*to imaginary viewers*). Ladies and... other ladies, this is unprecedented indeed. This is the first time the dish 'Nasi Kangkang' will be attempted on this programme. Known as a kind of magical love potion, this Southeast Asian-derived dish uses rice to make a man fall in love with you. 'A way to a man's heart is through his stomach', after all.

FATIMAH *mimics the action of stirring a pot.*

ALL. Double double toil and trouble. Fire burn and cauldron bubble. Fillet of a fenny snake –

LILY (*to imaginary viewers*). Unfortunately, we don't have the copyright to the words of the actual spell, so, sorry Mr Shakespeare, we have to misappropriate your words for now. But don't worry, we'll give you a step-by-step so that you can follow along. (*Beat.*) Now, put down that iron, ladies! Let's learn to cook!

FATIMAH. First, the woman must choose the man she want to control.

LILY. And what kind of man would that be?

FATIMAH. Oh, for example, if you think your husband cheat on you and you want him to fall in love with you again –

NISA (*interrupts*). That's very specific.

LILY (*to* NISA). It's just a hypothetical situation.

FATIMAH. Next, the woman must steam the rice –

NISA. Okay –

12. Literally means Crotch Rice, or rice over which someone has squatted.

FATIMAH. – and stand naked over the –

LILY (*to* FATIMAH). Whoa whoa whoa, Miss Fatimah, you have to slow down. Some people need some time to… follow along. (*To imaginary viewers.*) C'mon now ladies… Yes, yes, we don't need clothes for this dish. Yes. LIBERATE THOSE CLOTHES! EMANCIPATE YOUR BODY!

FATIMAH. Okay now, you stand with your – (*Gestures her groin.*) this one over the pot. Careful, it's a bit *panas*.[13]

LILY (*to imaginary viewers*). The heat from the steam will allow the sweat and vaginal juices to drip into the rice –

NISA. Gross! I don't think I want to do that.

LILY (*to* NISA). Don't worry, this is just a simulation. And please could you – (*Indicates for* NISA *to cover her mouth.*)

NISA *reluctantly covers her mouth.*

(*Smiling.*) It's much easier for everyone if you don't talk.

FATIMAH. Just cook like normal and once it is finished, the woman must give the rice to the man. If got some curry to eat with the rice, even better. After he eat, he will see her charm –

LILY. And will not go back to the dirty whoring slut he was seeing behind her back!

(*To* NISA.) Oh no, this is not about you. (*To imaginary viewers.*) Yes ladies, that's 'Nasi Kangkang', also known as 'Crotch Rice'! (*To* FATIMAH.) Kak, we might have gone too fast just now. Shall we repeat the steps for everyone out there?

FATIMAH *and* LILY *cover their mouths. The three ladies repeat the steps before in a kind of bizarre, dispassionate mime.*

After a while, NISA *uncovers her mouth and breaks the moment.*

NISA. Is this enough to make them listen?

LILY *uncovers her mouth.*

LILY. Yes. No one will judge us now. We are free to –

---

13. Hot.

NISA. To do what exactly?

FATIMAH *uncovers her mouth*.

FATIMAH. Say whatever we want.

   ***

LILY. The truth is –

NISA. They want the truth?

FATIMAH. They don't know they want, so we will give to them.

LILY. We owe it to ourselves. The truth is that we have to bend over backwards to be seen as equal.

NISA. But the truth is we can never be equal.

LILY. Yes, but we don't want to be equal to them at all. We want to be better than them. And who can blame us? We have been forgotten for so long.

FATIMAH. Yes, we must rise up!

LILY (*emboldened*). Yes, we must show them!

FATIMAH. No, I mean, with our voices only. (*Warning*.) Sisters, we cannot be so extreme.

LILY. Yes, we are not extremists.

NISA. Yes. I mean – no, we are not. We are moderate.

LILY. Yes, extremely moderate. We take the extreme position of the moderate zone.

FATIMAH. We're very close to the line. But we never cross the line.

NISA. Yes. I mean – no, we do not. We know where the lines are. We stay inside the lines. Where it's safe.

   ***

   LILY *takes* FATIMAH *and* NISA*'s hands*.

LILY. I'm glad to see you both again.

FATIMAH. Me too.

NISA. Me three.

Beat.

How long do you guys think it'll last?

FATIMAH. Last time, three days.

NISA (*recalls*). Oh yah. The first day, we ate till our bellies were full. The second day, we talked till our voices were hoarse. The third day, we danced till our legs wanted to break.

They laugh, remembering.

FATIMAH. Dancing girl. Mak used to call me that. I start in school at first, then the cabaret. My friend ask me to join with her and I said okay. Young, what? Later we become taxi girls.[14] Last time people thought taxi girls same like prostitutes, but actually I just dance only. I can do the cha cha, *ronggeng*,[15] the twist. All also can. Last time I wear miniskirt, hot pants. And my eyeliner, like Twiggy, you know? My waist was twenty-two inches that time. You believe? (*Beat.*) Now cannot lah, dance like that. You crazy? So old already. Later my husband kill me.

They remove the niqabs. They drink.

LILY. Too bad we won't be able to remember anything.

NISA. I wish we could. And you know, meet each other.

FATIMAH. How can.

NISA. I know.

They embrace each other.

Blackout.

---

14. Dancers in the 1950s and 1960s in Singapore who would dance with men for a fee at parties and clubs.
15. A type of traditional Malay dance step.

ACT TWO

The same room, the same furniture. Everything is back in its original place. It is not clear how much time has elapsed.

NISA, LILY *and* FATIMAH *are each standing around a table with their hands on their hips.*

NISA *is smiling confidently, looking out as she does so.*
LILY *and* FATIMAH *appear to be unsure about what they are supposed to do and look to* NISA *for guidance.*

All three hold their poses.

NISA (*to* LILY *and* FATIMAH). Okay, looking good, ladies. Now, if you do it right, you should start to feel the effects almost immediately.

LILY *and* FATIMAH *look at each other, communicating their skepticism silently.*

I know what you're thinking, ladies. Yes, power posing works. I used this that time when I successfully negotiated a ten per cent pay increase from my boss. Ten minutes before an important meeting is all you need! We usually focus on one pose a week, but we won't do that now, due to time constraints of course.

FATIMAH. Congratulations!

LILY. Yes, you should be proud.

NISA. Well, technically everyone got a raise. But I'm sure my negotiation helped. In some way. And because of me we all got free apples once every two months! Leftovers from the canteen. But still, better than nothing. So yes, I have had first-hand experience of the effectiveness of this method. And now...

NISA *puts her hands on the table with a bang that startles* LILY *and* FATIMAH. *The other two follow her actions.*

FATIMAH. Like this?

NISA. Open your legs a bit wider. (*Shouts.*) Wider!

LILY. Wow, you're really bossy when you're in teacher mode.

NISA. I know. It's like I'm a different person.

LILY. In my exercise class whenever we did squats, my instructor would say 'Ladies, imagine you've got testicles down there!' (*Adjusts her stance.*) And BAM! Manspread!

NISA. Exactly! Pretend you have a pair of balls between your legs.

FATIMAH (*chanting as she adjusts her stance*). Round round big big ugly balls…

The other two laugh in surprise.

What?

LILY. Gross! To be fair, I've seen my fair share of weird balls. Long ones, lopsided ones, hairy ones.

NISA. Channel that male sense of superiority. You can grunt if that helps you get into the mood.

They grunt.

FATIMAH. Like this?

NISA. Yes! Exactly! It's all part of creating that aura of power. You want to mimic that feeling of confidence, that self-belief that you want others to believe you have in you. It's not just aspirational thinking, ladies, but aspirational *being*.

LILY. But why do we have to pretend to be men?

FATIMAH. Cannot do woman pose? (*Adopts an exaggerated pose.*) Like, eh, look at my new expensive branded handbag.

LILY (*adopts an exaggerated pose*). Oh, what do we have here? It's just my super big diamond ring that you can never afford on your small salary!

FATIMAH (*accentuating her rear end*). Featuring… My FANTASTIC PANTAT![16]

LILY (*accentuating her breasts*). And guest starring… My HOT PATATAS TATAS!

---

16. Buttocks.

LILY *and* FATIMAH *move suggestively towards* NISA. NISA *squirms.*

What? Don't you like our sensual sexual aura dripping from our sexy sexy sex bodies?

NISA. You guys aren't taking this seriously.

LILY. Can't sexy mean powerful? When can being a woman ever be enough?

FATIMAH. Never.

NISA. I thought you two of all people would understand.

LILY. We do.

FATIMAH. We want to help only.

LILY. You think we don't want to be powerful? I don't want to be nothing, you know.

FATIMAH. Less than nothing.

NISA. All you do is complain! I'm so sick of this! Of these games. It's not –

NISA *accidentally knocks the table off balance. They freeze.* LILY *pauses, almost for effect. Then, the three women rattle off lines in a familiar, almost practised way.*

***

LILY. The babies! They're awake.

FATIMAH. Serves them right.

NISA. But they're screaming.

FATIMAH. Let them.

NISA. Shouldn't we do something?

FATIMAH. The younger they learn, the better.

LILY. Life is hard for a woman.

NISA. I can't bear to hear them crying...

LILY. Be strong.

NISA. For how long?

FATIMAH. For as long as it takes.

NISA. What if nothing changes?

LILY. We have to keep pushing.

    ***

FATIMAH (*to* NISA). You don't like to be here?

NISA. Of course. (*Beat*.) I love you both.

FATIMAH. Kakak like here. Here easy. Outside my head always
spin. (*Gestures 'spinning'*.) Like that. Need to think about
what to do. Need to cook, need to clean, need to wash, need to
iron. Need to think about what everyone need. Fulfil my
responsibility. Even when I have to do things I don't want.
(*Beat*.) Marriage is serious. I take it serious because I make
promise. I ask Allah for help so that I can do everything.
(*Beat*.) Sometimes it is painful. (*Beat*.) But I want everybody
to be happy. Then I also become happy. Then I can smile and
tell my children, 'Mak is happy.'

LILY. But what makes you happy, Kak?

*The song 'Knock Three Times' by Tony Orlando and Dawn
starts to play softly at first and then increases in volume. The
three ladies sing the chorus of the song.*

NISA. Kakak, your songs all so classic.

FATIMAH. Tony Orlando last time so handsome… his shirt
never button, can see the hair all… (*Remembers herself*.)
Astagfirullah hal adzim! God forgive me!

LILY. It's okay, Kak. We're here, remember? There's no one else.

LILY *retrieves the food and lays it on the table*.

FATIMAH. Still can eat?

NISA. Will it make us forget?

LILY. Yes. Yes, it will, my loves.

They eat in silence for a while.

So did you lose your virginity on your wedding night?

NISA *almost chokes*.

NISA. What?!

LILY. You and your husband. Did you –

NISA. I don't think that's appropriate to – .

LILY. Oh. Sorry. (*Beat.*) But like, 'same penis forever'. You know, like those balloons. You would think you guys would grow tired of – How do you put up with it?

NISA. Why are you –

LILY. Why do you put up with it? With him?

FATIMAH. Liy –

NISA *doesn't respond.* LILY *holds out a hand to* FATIMAH.

LILY. Have you confronted him about it?

NISA *doesn't respond.*

Have you confronted *her* about it?

Beat. NISA *stops eating.*

How can you –

NISA. What?

LILY. Stand it.

NISA. I just do.

LILY. And you're happy with the status quo?

NISA. I have it better than most.

LILY. You're not serious.

FATIMAH (*to* LILY). Liy, you don't understand. Sometimes, is easier.

LILY. To stay with men who treat you like crap?

NISA. It's more complex than that. We can't all be enjoying life.

LILY. What is that supposed to mean?

NISA. The meaningless sex. If you do it all the time with anyone, with no emotions –

LILY. You think I don't have emotions?

NISA. Well, not love, definitely.

LILY. What, the kind of love that takes a beating and keeps on
   going? (*Beat.*) Don't you think that I've been in love before?
   Maybe there's no romance, yes. But the act itself, is a, a
   moment of real… passion with someone. In that moment,
   I love him. All of them. For reaching deep into me and
   extracting that last bit of emotion that I have. That's why
   I give it so easily. My body. It's the only thing I have power
   over. It's powerful to feel needed. To know that I can cause
   a *reaction*. Even if it's just in a carnal, primal way, I am
   creating an effect. In that moment, I matter. And not for
   being a daughter, or a wife, or a sister. But just for being me.
   Is that so terrible?

FATIMAH. No.

NISA. No, it's terrible. We're all terrible. But we're just
   humans. What else can we do?

LILY. We are not *just* humans. We're more than that. That's
   why we're here.

FATIMAH. We must be more powerful…

LILY (*inspired*). Yes, we should be goddesses!

NISA. I don't understand. How can we –

   *There are sudden sharp cutting noises and lights. As they
   speak, they start to move differently and climb on top of the
   table. LILY retrieves three animal headpieces. They
   gradually put on these headpieces: FATIMAH – The Lion,
   NISA – The Goat, LILY – The Snake.*

LILY. Shhh… Don't make a sound. It's time for a story.
   Wouldn't you like that? Yes… shh… One day, there was
   a little girl. A dumb, stupid girl that no one wanted. She was
   cast aside the minute she was born. Her mother didn't want
   her, so she left her in a dirty *longkang*[17] to die.

FATIMAH. An old woman find the baby. Crying like a stupid
   baby. The old woman shoo away all the rats in the longkang.
   The baby her face so dirty and black from the longkang water.

LILY. Home was a rental flat filled with stale-smelling
   cardboard boxes. Against all expectations, the stupid girl

---

17. Drain.

lived, but the ugly woman died because she didn't have
a man that loved her and could take care of her.

FATIMAH. The girl don't know what to do. So she leave the
house before anyone do something bad to her. She walk and
walk until she see the longkang from last time. She go inside
the longkang.

LILY. It was dark and cold but she kept on walking because
there was nothing else to go back to. She saw a growing
brightness in the distance and a sound that was unlike
anything she had ever heard before.

FATIMAH. She walk to the very bright light and saw a big
animal. The big animal got three heads – head of lion, head
of goat, head of snake. All on one body. When it speak, fire
come out from all three of the mouth.

LILY. 'We are the body of three joined into one. We make men
shiver in their step. We make the seas rise and the earth
move. We are murder unto all men. We seek revenge for all
the women who have been wronged.'

FATIMAH. 'Actually you are supposed to die. But now you
will live forever. Find your two sisters and you will become
just like us.'

LILY. 'You will carry our spirit in you forever more. We will
always be there with you. Go.'

The three women fully form the Chimera.[18] *They radiate
strength.*

We can accomplish together what we cannot do alone.
Together, we are powerful.

NISA. I've never been so alive!

FATIMAH. So awake!

LILY. So unlike the women they expect us to be.

NISA. But what happens after?

*It becomes quiet suddenly, like a wave has just receded.
They come down from the table.* FATIMAH *removes her
headpiece.* NISA *and* LILY *follow suit.*

---

18. The Chimera, a hybrid Greek three-headed mythological beast comprising a
lion, a goat and a snake in one body, is said to strike fear in the hearts of men and is
generally considered a bad omen for them.

LILY. How can we achieve everything we're expected to achieve?
We are held to such a high standard. That's why I couldn't
justify the hijab any more. How could I? I was trying to get the
perfect ass at the gym while trying to also talk to God and
make him hear me. It felt hypocritical. I rebelled. I took it off,
and with it, all the restrictions I had put on myself. It wasn't the
cloth that was restricting me, no. It was like a lightning rod.
And the electricity came from all the people with their
wagging fingers telling me everything I was doing wrong.
I was wearing it wrong, or saying the wrong things, or bringing
shame to family. Once I removed it, I was completely free.

FATIMAH. We sacrifice more. That's why God rewards the
mothers.

NISA. What happens if you're not a mother?

FATIMAH. You have to at least try.

NISA climbs up the ladder and sits on the top step.

NISA. When I was young, we used to have this game. We'd
climb to the top of the stairs and dare each other to jump down.
First one step, then two steps – each time we'd add one more.
I used to be able to do thirteen. It was scary, but somehow
when you're young you can put aside your fears and fly and
land with this sense of thrill in your throat that's mixed up with
fear. It's exciting and your friends look impressed and you
beam with pride because you've gained some sort of power
with that one feat. I was better than the boys because I was
taller and had long legs. It was nice to beat them for a change.
As an adult, I tried to relive my past glories. I would stand on
the edge of the top step, but I was always filled with
a paralysing fear. My knees were no longer as strong as they
used to be. The concrete seemed harder. (*Beat.*) One day I tried
again. I fell, hard. I was four months pregnant.

FATIMAH. Girl or boy?

NISA. Girl.

FATIMAH. I'm sorry.

Beat.

LILY. But that's not what happened, right?

NISA *jumps off the ladder. There should be an element of danger to the jump.*

FATIMAH. It's easy to pretend. First time it happen, I thought my children don't know anything. Cos no scars. Cannot see blue-black on my body. After three days in the hospital, I come back and clean the house. Top to bottom. Like normal. I mop three times, then I cook dinner – lontong[19] with vegetables, tempe[20] and their favourite – bagedil.[21] I feed the cat. I bake banana cake. Inside I feel like so tired, but outside I am still their mother. I still have to feed them. I just say food poisoning. But they are my children. They know when Mak is in pain.

NISA. Why don't you just leave, Kak?

FATIMAH. Where can I go?

LILY. There's no need to be ashamed. Khadijah was a divorcee too, you know, before she met the Prophet.

FATIMAH. Peace and blessings be upon Him.

Beat.

I just want to talk and eat and sing and dance with you two.

LILY. We are here for you.

NISA. Is that enough? Being here for each other? How do we know that this isn't punishment? (*Beat.*) We are monstrous women. We allow others to treat us like monsters. Women are meant to be elevated. This is not like how God intended at all. We are so... subhuman.

LILY. You mean superhuman. A woman is designed – yes, by God, if you believe in Him – to withstand all the suffering she has to endure in her lifetime. If not, she builds a world for herself that's like this.

FATIMAH. Just like this one.

LILY. And fills it with everything she needs. Learn the ways to better protect herself next time.

FATIMAH. To keep going.

LILY. Before going back.

---

19. A Malay dish comprising rice cakes in spicy coconut gravy.
20. Fried fermented soybean.
21. A potato patty filled with mincemeat and spices.

FATIMAH. If she want to go back.

NISA. Why wouldn't she?

> LILY *looks at* FATIMAH, *and shrugs dismissively.*
> FATIMAH *tries to give* NISA *a hug, but* NISA *resists it.*

> This is bullshit. This isn't real. This place. Where women are
> instant best friends and support each other in everything they
> do. In real life we turn against each other all the time. I have
> half a mind never to come back here again.

LILY. We have to be in this together. Otherwise what's the
point? Remember all the women that fought for us before!
Like Joan and Marina and Maya, and Chimamanda and
Malala and Tarana![22] Don't let them die in vain!

FATIMAH. Some haven't die yet actually.

NISA. What is the point of reading all these books and theories
if you –

LILY. It's called being educated, Nisa.

NISA. You want to talk about education? Come, let's talk about
education. This is what I've learnt. I've learnt that we're born,
we get circumcised, our ears are pierced, we're told we're
Muslim and we're women, we should do this and do that and
we can't do this and we can't do that. What is the point? In the
end, we sin anyway and we're all going to hell. At least that's
what we're told. And I mean, we're the lucky ones. There are
some women who don't get to have a choice. Who they marry
or what jobs they have. Some don't get to be in control of their
own bodies. We don't all get to be feminists.

> *Beat.* LILY *takes a book, wipes the dust off its cover, then
> puts it back in its right place.*

LILY. I've been in love. He was a work colleague. Very geeky.
Very cute for an accountant. But it was just – it wasn't good
timing. He was married. (*Looks at* NISA *before continuing.*)
I was the one that ended it. Because I couldn't. Do it to her.
I know. I go on and on about female solidarity but – I would
have looked like the bad guy. Not him. I would have been
the homewrecker. She never found out though.

---

22. Feminist icons – French martyr Joan of Arc, Malaysian activist Marina Mahathir,
American writer Maya Angelou, and Tarana Burke, founder of the #MeToo movement.

NISA. Good for you. (*Beat*.) Look, that's shitty and you know it. But it's your life, I'm not going to stand here and judge you or call you a slut or whatever.

LILY. But I am a slut. A fucking, homewrecking slut. How do I live with myself?

NISA. What else can we do? Kill ourselves?

FATIMAH. Eh no, cannot.

NISA. No one would care even if we did.

LILY. I would care if you died. Kakak, you also. I would come to your grave and leave flowers for you both.

NISA. And how would –

LILY. You know how sometimes you walk by a cemetery, your eyes glaze over most of them? But then suddenly you somehow stop and see the names of one of them. Like, *really* see them. For no reason whatsoever?

FATIMAH. Kakak want yellow rose Liy, can?

LILY. Of course, Kak. (*Beat*.) I wonder if I'll go to heaven.

NISA. I thought you didn't believe in God.

LILY. I don't not believe in him. Sometimes I just question if he's there.

FATIMAH. If God is at home?

LILY. Yes! I feel like I'm ringing the doorbell, but God is… hiding behind the curtains. Like I'm trying to sell him encyclopaedias that he doesn't need.

FATIMAH. Or Tupperware!

They laugh, despite themselves.

LILY. Why doesn't he want to answer the door?

Beat.

NISA (*to* FATIMAH). Kakak, are we bad women? Is that why we're here?

FATIMAH. I don't know. Heaven and hell sometimes look the same like real life. You know, when I'm at home, Kakak like to sit in the kitchen and talk to Matahari.

LILY. The spy?

NISA. Who?

LILY. Mata Hari. The Dutch spy who used to live in Medan.

NISA *shrugs*.

FATIMAH. Oh I know that one! Very sexy one. She can do Javanese dance, you know.

LILY. They said that before she was killed, she blew a kiss to her executioner. A true femme fatale.

NISA. Stylish. (*To* FATIMAH.) Kakak, so which Matahari did you talk to?

FATIMAH. Matahari like the sun, because my cat her colour is orange. Very pretty. She like to sit inside the kitchen and look outside the window.

LILY. Oh! Ati likes to do that too while washing the dishes. She's always daydreaming. Sometimes I hear her singing.

FATIMAH. Matahari was very good. I *sayang*[23] her a lot. But now she's lost.

NISA. Lost how?

FATIMAH. She run away. Maybe cos in the house boring. Outside got birds, got other cats. Better lah.

LILY. Ati asked to go home at the end of last year and I said no. Because it's barely been a year and I'm scared that when she goes home, she won't want to come back again. That happens you know. Even when you don't treat them badly, they run. Why do they always run?

NISA. I don't want to hide any more, I don't –

LILY. What? Need us? You want to go back to your husband? You don't think he's found a way to comfort himself after all this time of you shutting him out?

NISA. Fuck you. You don't know anything. You're just a fucking slut that –

---

23. Love.

FATIMAH. Nisa –

LILY. Well, we only know what you tell us.

NISA. What do you want me to tell you? (*Beat*.) That there was no fall down some stupid steps? That it was just my stupid uterus? The stupid spare bedroom that I turned into a nursery and stupidly painted pink, and my stupid husband who didn't understand when I said, I needed time before we could try again, that I was scared, and stupid me who changed doctors twice because I didn't want to believe the first one, and all those stupid stickers people put on their cars that say 'Baby On Board' – I mean, what, do you think, people will magically drive better just because of a stupid sticker? What a joke! And the bigger joke is that we paid eight dollars for that stupid machine to merge our photos together to create a Frankenbaby that was just fucking hideous. A stupid monster baby I had to pretend I could love. When it's just my stupid less-than body that's preventing me from being whole. Is that what you want to hear?

A light from the back comes on. The women are bathed in darkness. We only see their silhouettes.

I named her Nur.[24] The light. I always dream that I can hear her crying, calling for me. Mummy's here, sayang. Mummy's sorry, sayang.[25] Don't cry any more, okay? You just go to sleep. Mummy will be here waiting for you.

LILY (*to* NISA). Shh shh… come here. You have us. You have us.

FATIMAH (*to* NISA). You will meet her again, Insya Allah.[26] She reserve place for you in heaven already.

FATIMAH *goes to hug* NISA.

NISA. What happens when we die? Do souls feel anything?

FATIMAH *doesn't respond.*

Is it painful like childbirth?

FATIMAH *doesn't respond.*

---

24. Arabic name meaning 'light' or 'illumination'.
25. My love.
26. God willing.

Will they will remember us?

FATIMAH *doesn't respond.*

Will they cry? Will there be tears of sadness, or regret?

FATIMAH *doesn't respond.*

What if I cannot bear it?

FATIMAH. You will. He has made you strong enough.

LILY *looks out into the light, searching.*

Blackout.

ACT THREE

The same room, with the same 'wine' bottle opened and glasses half-filled. It is still not clear how much time has elapsed.

All three women are holding glasses. They are all wearing their hair down. They are in the middle of a merry bout of drinking and playing the game Never Have I Ever.

LILY. Okay, never have I ever… kissed another girl.

> FATIMAH *drinks.* NISA *and* LILY *squeal.*

NISA. Kakak!

FATIMAH. What? Isn't it like this? (*Makes air kissing motion.*)

LILY. No Kak, it's like a real kiss.

FATIMAH. Oh. (*Beat.*) Also got.

NISA. Kakak!!

> FATIMAH *grins, enjoying the attention.*

> Okay okay… Never have I ever…. skinny-dipped in the ocean.

> LILY *drinks.*

FATIMAH. What is skinny-deep?

NISA (*to* FATIMAH). Swimming naked, Kak. No clothes. *Bogel.*[27]

FATIMAH. Oh!

> FATIMAH *drinks.*

LILY (*to* FATIMAH). Oh my God! Who are you!

FATIMAH. Last time at the *kampong.*[28] When I was young lah.

NISA (*to* FATIMAH). Okay Kak, your turn.

FATIMAH. I have never ever –

NISA (*to* FATIMAH). Never have I ever lah Kak!

27. Naked.
28. Village.

FATIMAH. Okay, never I have never –

They crack up.

I never… see before a black man's ber-bird![29]

LILY *drinks. They tease her.*

LILY. I see only lah, never touch!

They crack up. They top up their drinks and drink.

I feel like this is the bachelorette party that I'll never get to have.

NISA. You don't know that.

FATIMAH. God will help you find your soulmate, Lily.

LILY. Are you there God? It's me Lily. Ask my soulmate to find me okay? Cos I'm too fucking tired already.

NISA *retrieves three long white dresses, and they put them on. With their hair down, they resemble a pontianak.*[30]

Do I look like a bride!

FATIMAH. A bit.

NISA. Yah, a corpse bride.

They laugh. They roleplay a wedding ceremony.

LILY *stands in the middle, as if she is the bride, while* FATIMAH *and* NISA *stand to her side like bridesmaids.*

NISA *hums the 'Bridal Chorus' as they walk together, arms linked, towards the front of the stage.*

Once they reach the front, NISA *stands in front of* LILY *to be the officiator.*

FATIMAH *acts as the groom.*

NISA *takes* LILY*'s hand.*

NISA. I hereby declare that you, Lily Binte[31]… what's your father's name?

LILY. Doesn't matter.

---

29. Childish Singlish slang for a penis.
30. A Southeast Asian female ghost who is said to have died during childbirth.
31. Daughter of.

NISA. Okay, I declare you Lily Binte Doesn't Matter, are married to the Beansprouts Uncle[32] –

LILY. Eh!

They crack up.

Okay fine, I'm desperate. Beansprouts Uncle it is.

NISA. You are hereby married to the Beansprouts Uncle forever and ever until one of you decides that you have had enough of each other. May you have beautiful babies who will take care of you in your old age when you're useless and weak. *Amin.*[33]

FATIMAH. Amin!

NISA. You may now demurely kiss your groom's hand.

LILY *kisses* FATIMAH*'s hand, then licks it.*

FATIMAH. Ya Allah![34]

NISA (*to* LILY). Control yourself, woman!

FATIMAH. Come, we take picture.

The three of them take a selfie and look at the photo.

NISA. Wah, we really look like pontianak!

LILY. Shh! Don't say her name!

NISA. Then what? Kakak?[35]

LILY. Yah, better. She's like our big sister. (*To* FATIMAH.) Kak, you saw her before eh?

FATIMAH. Last time at the village got a lot of Kakak. Always at the banana tree there.

LILY. I've never liked ghost stories.

NISA. Don't be scared lah. Everyone thinks that the pontianak hates men. That we only target them when we come out at night. It's a common misconception. We don't hate men. We just want to scare them a little bit. We were scared, once. We used to be scared all the time.

***

32. An old man who sells beansprouts.
33. Amen.
34. Oh God. (An exclamation.)
35. Nickname for the pontianak is *Kakak* or big sister.

LILY. Walking home was scary.

FATIMAH. Or when got a lot of people.

LILY. People watching. Judging.

NISA. We only want them to feel a little of that fear.

FATIMAH. A bit only.

NISA. We don't go out of our way to haunt anyone.

LILY. The one that's haunted is us.

   ***

NISA. Remember the story about us taking the taxi to the graveyard with a white bundle in our hands that turned out empty? It was in that famous ghost storybook everyone used to read. Actually that story isn't scary. It's sad. We're just looking for our babies.

   LILY *pauses, almost for effect.*

LILY. I don't have one, though.

FATIMAH. Everyone got lose something.

   ***

NISA. A child.

FATIMAH. Love.

LILY. Innocence.

NISA. That we happen to look scary is purely coincidental.

LILY. Small matter.

FATIMAH. Some people say we eat men.

NISA. Oh, no.

LILY. Gross.

NISA. We just drive them a little crazy sometimes. Give them a small fever, things like that.

LILY. Yes, that's fun. I think I like being a ghost. We can never die. We'll always be around, lurking.

NISA. And we smell like jasmine.

   ***

LILY (*to* FATIMAH). Kak, is it true that the smell is stronger when she is near, and not so strong when she is far away?

FATIMAH. That's what people say.

LILY. I think I saw her once.

FATIMAH. Who?

LILY. I remember this sweet smell. Faint at first, then stronger and stronger. It was like she was filling me with every part of her. At one point, she came so close to me that I couldn't register her face. Everything was fuzzy. Her hair tickled. This black silk caressing my cheek. It wasn't really a hug. Too short for that, I didn't feel that warmth you get from a hug. But it felt like, like goodbye. I wish I could tell her 'Don't go.' 'Stay.' But I couldn't move at all and I did the only thing I could do, which was to cry, and then *Bapak*[36] came and picked me up against his shoulder. 'It was a bad dream, just a bad dream, sayang. Everything is okay now.' When you're young, you believe anything. Then you grow up and you know better. In the end you just wanna curl up into a ball in bed and cry and eat chocolate till you fall asleep.

NISA. Family, eh?

They laugh, almost feebly.

LILY. Neese – how many times do you think we've been in this place?

NISA. Twice, lah.

LILY. Guess again.

NISA. How long?

LILY. Kak Mah has been here for a while.

FATIMAH (*to* NISA). My children so big already. They don't want to spend time at home. People where got care about old woman like me?

LILY. Your mind has to find a way to occupy itself.

NISA. Kakak has been here the whole time?

LILY. Who do you think made the chicken?

---

36. Father.

FATIMAH *starts to put the food on the table.*

NISA (*to* LILY). And you?

LILY. On and off, for twenty years.

NISA. I don't understand –

LILY. My life sucks so I just like to check out once in a while.
Maybe if I start seeing a therapist she might say it's daddy
issues or something, but to tell you the truth, it could be
anything. The religious stuff, the family stuff... the sex.
Maybe it's just me. Maybe God didn't give me any
unscrewed-up parts that I needed to function normally as
a human being. (*Beat.*) I just end up feeling lost all the time.

NISA. And me?

FATIMAH. Not so many time.

LILY. A few times when you were still young, here and there.
A few more times in high school. Then nothing, until
recently. And you kept coming back.

NISA. But why can't I remember?

FATIMAH *and* LILY *don't answer.*

NISA *looks at the bottle on the shelf.*

I thought you said it doesn't have alcohol.

LILY. It doesn't. We're all very lucid here. This is just your
body's way of protecting yourself. We find that with some
girls, it's better not to remember.

NISA. There are others?

FATIMAH. A lot.

LILY. There are many rooms like this. Some have it harder than
us. Some, like Kakak, prefer to be here instead of out there.
Some don't remember which world is the real one.

NISA. Isn't that bad?

LILY. Depends. One could argue that reality is only an illusion.
I know. It's messed up. But I also think the existence of this
space is a thing of great beauty. We created it to preserve our

inner essence. What makes us special. No one can touch that if we keep it in a box like this.

FATIMAH *lies down on the sofa.*

But there are some happy endings. The ones who leave and never return. It's bittersweet when we have to say goodbye.

NISA. So one day I could maybe leave forever, too?

FATIMAH. Yes. Insya Allah, can.

LILY. Possibly.

Beat.

NISA. Fuck men, you know. Fuck them. All of them. Who needs them?

LILY (*half-amused*). Yeah, fuck them.

FATIMAH (*sitting up*). But not all, right? Some nice.

LILY. Some nice. But sometimes all.

FATIMAH (*nodding*). Sometimes all.

LILY. Without a common enemy, we'd never agree on anything. It's like when I used to wear the hijab. It was the women's opinions that bothered me the most. Some of my best friends were suddenly 'so worried' that I was being 'oppressed' by the men in my community. There were the ones who criticised how I was wearing it – too trendy, too old-fashioned. And they scrutinised the other parts of my body too. Too tight, too short. It became so ridiculous. And when I decided to remove it, there was flak about that too. It was all very hypocritical. I decided that I couldn't be bothered any more.

NISA. How can we bring life into this world? This fucking hard world.

LILY. I don't know. (*Beat.*) Every time I get my period, I'm secretly happy. I just want to empty my body out completely, until there's nothing left. (*To* FATIMAH.) Kak, does God hate me?

FATIMAH. No. God loves all His children. He only tests you because He knows you can take it.

LILY (*wrily*). He must think we're fucking strong then.

Beat.

The babies.

NISA. What? Oh! They're not crying!

LILY. It's time.

NISA. I don't understand.

FATIMAH. Time to go?

LILY. We're free.

NISA (*to* FATIMAH). Kak, you want to go?

FATIMAH. If you all go, I go.

LILY (*to* FATIMAH). Where will you go, Kak?

FATIMAH. I want to go to East Coast Beach. I want to feel the sea water on my body. Salty, like tears. I want to see my children and tell them I love them.

NISA. I love you both. I hope to never see you here again.

LILY. Me too.

FATIMAH. Me three.

NISA. So I won't remember any of this?

LILY (*to* NISA). Maybe you might get glimpses, in those spaces just before you fall asleep. But it won't feel as long. Sometimes what feels like days here are only minutes there.

FATIMAH. Want to eat?

NISA. One last meal, shall we, sisters?

They retrieve the food.

LILY (*chewing*). Mmm… Good, right?

Beat.

FATIMAH. Got one night, I go downstairs to the playground. Like 2 a.m., 3 a.m. I don't want my children to see. Got nobody so I sit at the swing. I swing, swing. I feel like I am

like a child again. And you know, I saw Matahari. She so big
already. 'Matahari, come here sayang.'[37] And she come to
me. She rub-rub her body on my leg. And I happy. I happy
she is okay.

NISA. Tomorrow is a new day. A new dawn.

LILY. And yesterday?

Her question is unanswered.

The song 'Knock Three Times' plays.

Let's go after this.

FATIMAH. Tony Orlando. My favourite.

NISA. I'll never get sick of it.

They continue eating. The song gets louder.

Beat.

What can be seen: The room, all the furniture.

*Three women, NISA, LILY and FATIMAH, are standing in
the middle of the space. They do not notice one another.*

Spotlights on each of them to reveal the following:

*NISA is stirring a cup of coffee. She sits down and sips from
her cup.*

*FATIMAH is cleaning a table. When she is done, she takes
a seat.*

*LILY is trying on a silk hijab as she watches a video on
her phone.*

*Someone knocks on the door. Three knocks. All three women
stand up, like they are about to get the door.*

What we do not see: who is at the door.

Blackout.

End.

---

37. Matahari, come here my love.

JERICHO

MALAPROP Theatre

MALAPROP THEATRE

MALAPROP Theatre is a Dublin-based collective of theatre-makers. We aim to challenge, delight, and speak to the world we live in (even when imagining different ones). Works include *LOVE+*, *BlackCatfishMusketeer* by Dylan Coburn Gray, *JERICHO*, and *Everything Not Saved*. Log on to malaproptheatre.com and/or @malaproptheatre for more info and upcoming performance dates.

–

JERICHO was commissioned by Bewley's Café Theatre, Dublin, and premiered there in February 2017. It was then reworked and performed at Underbelly as part of Edinburgh Festival Fringe 2018, and at VAULT Festival, London, on 6 February 2019. The cast was as follows:

M	Maeve O'Mahony
J	John Gunning
CARL	Ronan Carey
DAVE	John Doran
ALICE	Breffni Holahan
JM	Jack Toner
D	Deirdre Van Wolvelaere
Director	Claire O'Reilly
Devised by	Dylan Coburn Gray
	Claire O'Reilly
	Maeve O'Mahony
	John Gunning
Dramaturg	Breffni Holahan
Poster, Set, Costume Design	Molly O'Cathain
Lighting	John Gunning
Sound and AV Design	Claire O'Reilly
Producer	Breffni Holahan
Associate Producer	Carla Rogers

With thanks to Ciaran and all at Culture Ireland, Colm, Kelly, David and Iseult at Bewley's Café Theatre, Sara Gannon, Cate Russell, Emer Casey, Suzie Bennett, Eoghan Quinn and Kevin Owens (not).

Characters

M, *a journalist in her twenties/early thirties*
J, *M's housemate, a burgeoning ASMR artist*

CARL, *a journalist*
DAVE, *a journalist*
ALICE, *a journalist and M's boss*
JM, *wrestling podcast presenter*
D, *wrestling podcast presenter*
MAM, *M's mother*
ROLAND BARTHES

Note on Text

The text in bold is not necessarily spoken live on stage. In our version, it was a combination of voiceover and projection, but it's up for grabs.

It's also worth noting that while M is a journalist and J is her housemate, they are also theatre-makers making the show. M references this early on, and J operates the show throughout. This isn't important in a narrative sense, but an awareness of it in production probably is.

As we say near the start of *JERICHO*, it's hard to stay up to date. Because of Stuff, and how it keeps happening. The world is never not changing. The text published in this collection is the version performed at Underbelly as part of Edinburgh Fringe Festival 2018. It's set in Ireland in July 2018 and reflects our thoughts and concerns as of then.

ENTRANCES

J presses a button and we hear the kind of grandiose music you might hear when a procession enters a church. He can make amicable short or non-verbal responses to M throughout.

M enters looking dubious. She indicates to J to cut the music.

M   Ehm –
Yeah.
But –
No, though?
I see what you mean –
I mean, I see where you're coming from –
But, when I said 'entrance' –
I didn't mean that kind of –
I meant more of a, y'know, rousing, charged –
d'yaknowwhatImean?

J indicates he knows what M means.

Okay!
Cool!
Let's go!

M exits. J plays a song from a musical. M re-enters with more enthusiasm than last time, but it's not quite right. Again, she indicates to cut the music.

Yes, yes, okay –
I see what you did there –
Yeah –
Charged, rousing music –
Yes, I get it –
And I know you love that musical –
Thanks, yeah –
But if we could go less musical-y and recognisable, that'd be great –
Just more energetic and, like –

J indicates again that he knows what M means.

Okay.
Cool.
Right.

M *exits once again. J plays dance music. M re-enters and really gives this song a go, but it's just not what she's looking for. She indicates to J to stop the music.*

Yeah, yeah –
I mean –
Absolutely bangin' tune –
No doubt about that –
But a bit too –
Let's go less 'club' and more '*arena*', y'know?

J *indicates that this time he really knows what* M *means.*

And, if you could, would you mind adding a bit of crowd noise?
I just need a bit of –
Not that you guys aren't great, it's just –
I need a bit of a lift, y'know?
Great, thanks.

THIS IS JERICHO

M *exits. J plays 'Break the Walls Down' by Fozzy.*

M *enters triumphantly.*

M   WELCOME. TO. JERICHO!
At this point, I feel I should clarify:
This show is not called JERICHO because of the wrestler.
It's a fair assumption, what with –
you know –
all this.
But it's called JERICHO after the city.
The ancient city in modern-day Palestine that dates back to the very first settled humans, at the beginning of agriculture.

If not the oldest city, then the oldest city with a
protective wall to keep out people you don't want in
your city.
Which Chris Jericho's signature move and song are
named after.
Which just goes to show.
The fact that they *had* a wall, not that there's a wrestling
move named after it.
The wall.
The wall goes to show, the wrestling move doesn't go
to show:
That some things don't change.

Have we any wrestling fans in tonight?

Maybe there is. Maybe there isn't.

Some people think that agriculture was the beginning
of this amazing graph.
The graph is us.
Humanity.
Always moving up and away from hunting giant ground
sloths and gathering berries and dying in childbirth more
often than not towards more glorious futures.

But, actually, hunting giant ground sloths was pretty
great.
As soon as people start farming the fossils get
noticeably smaller due to malnutrition, due to their less
diverse diet.
Ten thousand years ago bread made us all short and sad.
Which just goes to show.
Some people think it's the opposite.
They think it's all been downhill since farms, because
we've been steadily losing touch with nature and the
delicate balance of tendencies that allows us to exist at
all in the first place.
But, actually, hunting giant ground sloths was pretty
shit from the giant ground sloths' perspective.
America only has plains because early humans burnt
down huge swathes of forest in order to drive game.
Early humans may have had a profound relationship
with nature, but it expressed itself as 'Fuck giant
ground sloths'.

We were asked to make a show about the world.
Which is tough.
Where do you begin?
We briefly thought that would be the title.
Where Do You Begin?
We also thought we might call it 'The Bends' but then
we remembered that that's a Radiohead album.
Where the fuck *do* you begin?
What is there to say?
That is, what is there for us, a theatre company from
Ireland, a town on the edge of Europe in the grander
scheme of things, to say?

Even considering recent progress we've made on gay
marriage and extremely recent progress we've made
on female reproductive rights, we have to remind
ourselves that we only made that progress now because
we hadn't made it already.

And we look at other nations who made it twenty, thirty,
forty years ago and can now feel it slipping away.

So where does that leave us?
And what is there for us to say?
But the alternative is to remain silent.

Because that's the problem, isn't it?
To look away is obscene.
But to say something just to be seen to be saying
something is also obscene.
If not *more* obscene.
And to spend enough time learning what you would
need to have learnt in order to say something that
hasn't already been said would be absurd.

As a journalist, it's something I wrestle with every day.
That's not a joke.

Because you need that time in order to do the work
that pays the bills and rent or mortgage.
Existing is expensive.
Even if you manage to educate yourself, you'll only be
educated for five minutes.
And then you'll fall behind anyway, because of Stuff.
And how it keeps happening.

Like, all the time.
Knowing about the world is an investment.
And it's not one you can afford.

So, where *does* that leave us?

And where is it all going?
Maybe rather than say something you connect some
things.
Maybe art's job isn't to create, but to make you realise
what you already know but don't know you know,
y'know?

When Journalism's Art, maybe Art has to be
Journalism.

BREAKFAST ASMR

M *watches* J. *We're now in their kitchen.*

J   Hey guys.
            I've had a lot of requests for this.
            So here we go.
            This is Kellogg's Corn Flakes.

            J *pours a bowl of Corn Flakes, adds milk, and begins*
            to eat them. This action is deliberately done into two
            mics. He is recording the audio for his ASMR YouTube
            channel. M *continues to watch him.*

M   Will you put the bins out tonight please?

            J *makes a gesture indicating he can't talk right now.*

            Oh sorry.
            The bins.
            The bins?
            The BINS.

            J *gives a thumbs-up.*

            Thanks.
            Chewing? Is that a thing?

J *gives an affirmative shrug.*

M *receives a text from her* MAM. *We can read it too.
It's littered with inappropriate emojis.* M *doesn't
respond.*

MAM   **Hiya young thing I just hit a deadline glass of wine
in order tonight!!! Hope you are keeping well... I
won't say busy... learned my lesson!... shout if you
want to get coffee or dinner soon... MAM**

*PS What is Cunt Magic

RUNNING

M *runs.*

M   I'm running to my office.
I'm not running because I hate myself.
I'm not running because I'm a health freak.
I'm not running to lose weight so that strangers on the
internet will look at me and think 'Wow, she conforms
to societal beauty standards. She must eat a lot of
avocados.'
I'm running so I don't gain weight.
I'm running to stay where I am.
Because that's how that works.
If you spend five days a week sitting at a desk, you
have to run to stay where you are.
I'm running to the office of the one-syllable-name
content aggregator that I work for.
In the context of digital journalism, a one-syllable-
name is non-threatening, 'matey'.
We cover issues of Class and/or Gender, as well as
videos of cute cats or babies doing those things they
do, but we have an arm's-length relationship with
Statistics, I mean, doesn't everyone?

When we're on the clock, we have to produce a story
every forty-five minutes.

Given a 'story' is just two hundred words about an interesting thing on the internet that's yet to peak in popularity, like the cats or the babies, it's actually more doable than it sounds.

But there are also meatier, reseachier, featurier affairs. Bigger word count, bigger share range, bigger reach. Only, we get those assigned to us by Alice, who isn't the leader our horizontally organised workplace full of beanbags doesn't have.

And so far I've been granted such groundbreaking topics as The Top 10 Disney Characters You Couldn't Have a Dinner Party Without and Blind Date to Blissful Devotion: Cilla Black's Legacy Lives on Through Love.

Not ideal.

But you know, stepping stones. You have to start doing something somewhere.

Because that's how that works.

Some things won't happen in the future unless they start happening now.

OFFICE 1

M *arrives at her office in time for a meeting with her colleagues* ALICE, DAVE *and* CARL. *They should be a bit unnatural, maybe subtly overbearing.*

ALICE   **So um –**
The first assignment is –
It's um –
Just a mo –
Oh, yeah –
An upcoming marathon for a form of cancer less popular than breast cancer and –
I mean eh –
What was I –
Because –
Dave, you can take this; you're in to running right?

DAVE   No, yeah –
        Just a quick question –
        I forget my question, but –
        Just, yeah, I'll take this.

M   Dave always has a quick question he always forgets.

ALICE   Okay, secondly, an Irish politician has said a thing
        about women like you can generalise about women.
        But, y'know, like –
        That's, well –
        Just, y'know –
        Very –
        You can't
        So, the second one's on that and the, like –
        The, eh –
        Ongoing coverage as he tries to backtrack.
        So, the best person for the job is... Carl.

CARL   Yeah, like –
        No bother, like, considering –
        Just, y'know, 'feminist man' and all, like,
        d'yaknowtheway?

        M *makes a face.*

ALICE   Okay and saving the best for last,
        The third's a piece on –
        Well, it's –
        It's –
        So MASSIVE Ireland and UK WWE tour this
        winter –
        And with the sort of –
        What are they –
        Aw, no, I had it, but –
        So, that plus gas tie-ins from the archive in the
        run-up to rebuild our wrestling-fan traffic –
        Like, um, the thing that the –
        When they all are all –
        We don't have a wrestling archive.
        But do you know what I mean?

M   Yeah, okay, cool.

I never know what Alice means, I just make positive
noises until the agony ends.

Wrestling. Amazing. So more specifically –

ALICE   **Don't overthink it hun.**
      Seriously.
      Like, I just mean go learn gas stuff about wrestling
      like that time the boss had a feud with literal God
      and challenged him to a, what's it even called?,
      a duel?, that people will click on.
      Y'know?
      Or when that huge guy pretended to be that other
      huge guy pretending to fuck a corpse.
      Not that that's gas to me but y'know –

M   **Of course. Gas. That's me. You can call me the...**
      gasman.

      *M's colleagues fake-laugh. M cringes and goes to
      speak again, but they all start talking over her.*

      Although always being positive even though you're
      always confused is pretty agonising in and of itself.

ALICE   **Okay everyone, back in the room. I'm looking at**
      you, Carl!

CARROT ASMR

M is back home, talking to J with a raw carrot in hand.

M   Do you know what, I don't even want to write about
      that politician.
      Even feminist stuff in general –
      Pay and violence and –
      Actually pay and violence pretty much covers it,
      bleak –
      And anyway it's exhausting because it's all the time.
      Someone's always just been murdered by statistically
      their husband or their boyfriend –

But also sometimes a stranger because only the
depressing clichés are true –
Besides, I'm not the best person for the job, because
that's Carl.

M *bites the carrot.*

I know wrestling is not the worst topic.
Roland Barthes wrote an essay on wrestling.
I haven't read it, I just know it exists.
All I mean is it's not getting me any closer to my
Pulitzer.
By the way, I don't know if you have food plans but
I'm not going to cook tonight so you won't be able to
benefit from my shit portion management.
Fair warning!
I'm not dieting.
I just feel like my current diet is a moral failing of mine.
Working through lunch and just eating biscuits.
Fuck me.

J *notices the crunching sound.*

J   Would you mind –

M   Oh you want me to – okay cool.

         M *bites the carrot into the mic. She does loud
         obnoxious cartoon chewing.*

J   Just normally. Just eat the carrot.

         It's like two ears. That's how you get the response. So,
         like, both mics.

         M *moves from one mic to the other, chewing.* J *gives a
         thumbs-up.* M *stops.*

M   Obviously I know I'm not going to win a Pulitzer.
         I'm not American.
         And I'm not incredibly talented.
         I don't know, Pulitzer just means making enough
         money by working.
         Because no one does any more except superstars,
         which is fucking crazy.
         Or even just not getting further into debt.

Like I hope this isn't rude, but this place is too nice for
what we're paying for it and it's still too expensive,
how are you surviving with – I don't know what's a
good number of subscribers, six hundred?

J   Thousand?

M   What?

J   That's a good number yeah.

M   Seriously?

J   As in are there channels like that?

M   With that many, yeah.

J   Loads. People like relaxing.

M   Yours?

J   Getting there.

M   And it's definitely not a sex thing?

J   Everything is a sex thing to someone.

M   True.

J   It's not primarily. I reckon I could get another fifty
thousand subs if I did anime big-brother incest, but
I let my parents throw me a few bob towards our rent
instead.

M *receives a text from her* MAM.

MAM   **What is cunt magic**
             ?
             MAM

M   So there's at least eight things to ask about there, but
let me just...

M *indicates that she has important phone business to
attend to, and leaves.*

Alone in her bedroom, M *replies.*

**Stupid internet joke, it's a way of saying someone
is feminine and resilient and clever in an
understated way**

MAM   **Does Marilyn Monroe have cunt magic
       ?
       Cunt magic
       Cunt Magic
       It looks better with capitals**

M   **You'd say Marilyn Monroe is pure Cunt Magic not
       she has it**

MAM   **Marilyn Monroe is pure Cunt Magic!!!**

RESEARCH

M *tries to write her article but has no idea where to start.*

M   WWE is… WWE is… Anyone? Anyone at all? Roland
       Barrrrrrthes?

       *She watches an interview with Roland Barthes. His
       French answers are translated deliberately incorrectly
       with the following English subtitles.*

RB   **It no longer matters whether the passion is genuine
       or not.
       What the public wants is the image of passion, not
       passion itself. There is no more a problem of truth
       in wrestling than in the theatre.
       The joy of wrestling is certainty,
       the certain knowledge that André the Giant is good
       and Thauvin bad,
       People like deciding what's good and what's bad
       even if it doesn't make sense.
       Capitalism good communism bad,
       marriage good infidelity bad,
       heterosexuality good and having sex with a
       beautiful undergrad boy who says he loved your
       novel bad, even if you don't ghost him because it
       turns out he unironically likes Sasha Velour more
       than Shea Couleé,
       white good because the empire never happened and
       black bad because biology,**

**male good because muscles and female bad because
berries,
Irish good because we never had an empire we just
stamped the paperwork of slavery, abortion bad
because a sperm is half a baby meaning a fertilised
egg is definitely a whole baby.**

M   Thank you Roland, I am now even more confused
than I was before. I think I may take a more traditional
route.

This is the bit of the story where I google WWE and
read the entirety of the WWE Wikipedia page because
I am a good journalist.

M *gives a thumbs-up.*

I learn faces are handsome good guys who normally
look like locals. Or what people think locals look like.
They're sometimes called Blue-Eyeses in the UK,
interpret that as you see fit.

I learn heels are lumpy bad guys who tend to be
foreign, because as we all know foreigners love to hit
you with steel chairs when they haven't even been
tagged in. Irish heels are often Unionists or Anglo-Irish
landlords or British. No comment.

I learn about fans having signs and chants so you can
always tell who's just like you and who's a total
fucking weirdo.

I learn about kayfabe, which means knowing wrestling
isn't real but not caring, because the way you feel
when you wave your sign and chant your chant with
everyone else who is JUST. LIKE. YOU. is more
important than the stupid fucking truth.

Who needs the truth when you finally belong?

M *goes deep into a wrestling YouTube hole.
Eventually, a wrestling podcast plays.* JM *and* D *are
the presenters.*

JM   **Like, reasons why I watch wrestling: I like how
wrestlers look is up there.**

D   Yeah.

JM   Sure, I think that, like, athleticism is cool, and I like
         the women, I like how kind of progressive it can be
         in a weird way if you don't… if you squint real
         hard… I like… I like… Eh… I like a bunch of stuff.
         But one thing I will never like as much as Vince
         McMahon is just like 'Aw, look at him there with
         his big muscles and his tiny little shorts. Aw, make
         him jump on top of that other big muscly guy and
         his tiny little shorts. Alright!' He started out as, like,
         a small-time promoter on the east coast, and
         actually it wasn't even him. It was his dad. He
         inherited the business.

D   Yeah.

JM   But, ultimately, he's just Starbucks.

D   Yeah.

JM   He's just someone that was able to buy up all the
         competition and then… Just… He's… All of a
         sudden, he's so big that no one will ever have a
         chance of touching him.

         And… And the one… And, like, how does that
         family actually function? Like, does Vince
         McMahon actually love his kids? There have been
         so many plotlines that would lead you to believe he
         doesn't. But they're a family business and their
         family is business. There's no family left there. It's
         so fucking creepy. This is a guy that will not let you
         sneeze around him 'cause he sees sneezing as a sign
         of weakness. This guy is not an easy guy to say no
         to, so no one fucking says no to the guy –

         No, but the family is absolutely fucked. Like,
         there's no way that a father could look at his
         daughter as a sixteen-year-old girl and say 'You
         know what storyline I want to write? I want to say
         "Uh this will make the fans really mad!" I'm gonna
         fuck my daughter.' This is a plot that he tried to lay
         out: 'I'm gonna fuck my daughter. She's gonna get
         pregnant. There's gonna be a whole incest angle for,

**like, years. We're gonna have a little fucking baby
out on this ring and the baby's gonna get suplexed
on some shit.' This is how this guy thinks.**

**I mean, how many little wrestlers, how many
families, how many terrible messages have to get
out of this fucking company before people actually
say maybe we shouldn't let a guy who came to
power as a fucking oligarch in the middle of this
territory system, to continue running a business?
How many broken fucking promises? Where is my
WWE ice cream? Where is my CM Punk return?
Where is any of the things that all of the fans who
actually give their fucking time, their fucking
money, to ever gonna come?**

M   And then they stop.
     They stop streaming.
     My apartment goes quiet.
     It's a bit of a shock, that sudden quiet.
     A seagull makes a seagull noise.
     I didn't think they'd just stop.
     But then, why not just stop?
     Why keep going if you're just going to get more and
     more upset?
     It's not healthy to push on.
     I mean, obviously there are cases.
     Where you have to.
     Push on.
     But if you can just stop, why not just stop?
     Stop streaming.
     Stop driving.
     Stop flying.
     Stop telling zodiac quiz sites your home address.
     Stop retweeting things morons say just because it's
     moronic.
     Stop watching wrestling.
     Stop giving your time and, implicitly, *money* to
     fucked-up industries that only exist because of people
     giving them time and, implicitly, money.
     Stop so that it'll all stop.
     Isn't that comforting?
     That if we switch off, it'll eventually stop happening.

OFFICE 2

M *is back in her office.*

CARL   **Hey hey hey hey hey hey hey!**

M   **Hi Carl.**

CARL   (*Terrible Chris Jericho impression.*) **You just made the list!**

M   **As in – ?**

CARL   **The List!**

M   **Chris Jericho's?**

CARL   **He's a really famous wrestler.**

M   **Never heard of him.**

CARL   **Seriously?**

M   **No, I just said his name.**

CARL   **Oh.**

M   **Joking**.

CARL   (*Lying badly.*) **Me too!**

M   **What was your joke?**

CARL   **Telling you something you already knew.**

M   (*Lighthearted josh.*) **Such a MAN.**

CARL   (*Not really joshing.*) **How DARE you it was IRONIC.**

M   **How's your piece?**

CARL   **I'm feeling a lot of feelings. Women have such a shit time.**

M   **They do.**

CARL   **I feel like I should chop my willy off.**

M   **I can't tell if you're joking.**

CARL   **Me neither.**

M   Carl wants to be an internet-famous funny young Irish
         journalist.
         Failing that, I think he wants to kill internet-famous
         funny young Irish journalist Carl Kinsella and wear his
         skin, to punish him for having been funny and called
         Carl first.
         I think he thinks internet-famous people have pensions.
         Carl needs to sleep more and tweet fewer nostalgic
         jokes about Pokémon Red.

         M *receives another text from her* MAM.

MAM   **Let me know about dinner love, it's on me... MAM
         Money smiley**

HEADLINES

At some point throughout this section, we leave the office.

M   I've just written a story about a lad from Leitrim who
         has thrown a bag of rice at his mother every day for the
         last five years. **Unbelievable! Leitrim Legend
         Throws Basmati Rice at his Mam Every Day for
         Five Years**

         I'm currently reading a story about the latest powerful
         image of a Syrian child that encapsulates something of
         the horror of the situation over there. She is at most
         four, and shrapnel has torn a lump of flesh the size of
         an adult thumbprint out of her cheek, like some
         obscene finger-painting. The bright flow of blood
         across her otherwise filthy face is stark. Cinematic,
         almost. **Latest Syria Attacks Leaves Twelve Dead**

         I'm just about to start on a story about a video of a cat
         that can meow such that it sounds not unlike it's
         singing 'I Will Always Love You' by Whitney
         Houston. **You Won't Believe Who's Been
         Reincarnated as This Cat!**

Now there's a story about coastguards abandoning migrants

J   **Libyan coastguard accused of abandoning three migrants in sea**

M   Now there's a story about Hillary

J   **Twenty-five Million Votes for Clinton 'Completely Fake' – She Lost Popular Vote**

M   Now there's a story about kangaroos

J   **The Sad Reason Kangaroos are Acting Drunk**

M   Is that a real thing?
      Now there's a story about the Queen sending coded messages

J   **Was the Queen sending coded messages to Donald Trump via her brooches? Absolutely**

M   Is that one real? Don't worry, we're not going to turn the house lights on. Just for yourself, was that real?
      Now there's a story about Siri heckling the Defence Secretary

J   **Siri 'Heckles' British Defence Secretary Gavin Williamson in the Middle of Parliament Speech**

M   Real, yes or no?
      Now there's a story about a wrestler that once burned another wrestler alive inside a casket drenched in gasoline

J   **WWE's Kane is the New Mayor of Knox County Tennessee**

M   Is that real?
      Now there's a story about Obama banning the National Anthem

J   **Obama Signs Executive Order Banning the Pledge of Allegiance in Schools Nationwide**

M   What about that one?
      Is this real?

J   **Boris Johnson licks Avicii's coffin**

M   What about this one?

J   **Trees**

M   What about this one?

J   **Alligator eats boy trying to impress teenage girl**

M   What about this one?

J   **In the time it took you to read this, Elon Musk kicked a swan**

M   Sometimes real doesn't mean true.
Real doesn't always mean it happened.
Real just means someone wrote this and then people read them.
Though in that sense, they're all real because you're reading them.
In that sense, real just means whatever we're talking about.
In that sense, whatever we don't talk about can't be real.
An event you don't talk about didn't happen.
A crime you don't talk about wasn't committed.
A mass grave you don't talk about doesn't exist.

We invented the 'cunt magic' meme for this show.
And you now understand it, whether you want to or not.
And we've now put these headlines in your head, whether you wanted them or not.
If you see an article in three hours' time saying Elon Musk kicked a swan, it'll be familiar rather than shocking.
Even if you see an article saying Elon Musk DIDN'T kick a swan, you'll think he did something.
Whereas maybe he did nothing.
We've killed the possibility that Elon Musk did nothing.
Just by talking.
Talking kills.
But not talking kills too.
So where does that leave us?
And where is it all going?

M *and* J *look at each other for a while before* J *inhales deeply and blows a raspberry into his mics.*

J   Sorry, that's probably not helpful.

M   No, actually it's kind of nice.

        J blows a few more raspberries while M *gets a packet*
        of biscuits from her bag and gives the audience a
        'don't judge me' look. Maybe she offers someone one.
        J *stops.*

TROLL

M *is back at home late into the night before her article is due.*

M   Suddenly, the assignment is due tomorrow. This. This
        is still everything I've written.

        Suddenly, my research-related tabs are narrowing to
        make room for non-research-related tabs.

        Suddenly, I'm reading an article on a specific brand of
        right-wing politics that gives definitions of words I've
        never heard of used by people I've never met.
        Suddenly, I'm reading the response to this article
        written by a well-known feminist journalist,
        denouncing the first article and its definitions and the
        institution that published it.
        Suddenly, I'm reading the institution's response to the
        response, justifying why they published the first article
        at all.
        Suddenly, I'm halfway through the packet of biscuits.
        Suddenly, I'm reading the comments under the
        response to the response, which is arguably the internet
        equivalent of injecting hydrofluoric acid up your
        own nose.

        Suddenly, one of the comments makes me
        involuntarily spit a lump of biscuit on my laptop
        screen, right where the guy who made the comment's
        name and picture are, because they've used the word
        'rapefugee' like that's a real word that refers to a real
        thing, which it isn't and doesn't.

Suddenly, I'm replying to Lumpy Biscuit, because
even if it's not a real word, I resent that they think it is.
Suddenly, Lumpy Biscuit replies to me.
Suddenly, I think Lumpy Biscuit is too kind a
nickname for this prick.
Suddenly, a lot of time has passed, I'm on my sixth
reply, which is five hundred and seven words longer
than what I've written for my actual job this evening,
and the tea is very cold, and the apartment is very dark,
and the packet is very empty, and I have crumbs on my
face, and my lap, and, arguably, my soul, *but* my
replies have a total of thirty-four likes and Lumpy
Biscuit only has eleven.
Suddenly, this makes me feel giddy and powerful.
Suddenly, I am the queen.

The wrestling match to end all wrestling matches
ensues between M and J. J is now dressed as Lumpy
Biscuit.

Suddenly, I imagine that I am in fact the Queen, well a
queen, and my followers and I form a glorious holistic
commune with equal opportunities and nomadic
tendencies and frequent orgies that are somehow both
graceful and unintimidating.

Suddenly, Lumpy Biscuit's cohort storms our
community with their hate and their fear and their
slippery non-sequiturs we can't spear with reason.

Suddenly, the Eden evaporates and we're in a
conference centre, full of haze and strobe and BO and
repressed homosexuality, home to this spectacle for
one night only, and I'm leaping off the ropes of the
ring to land a nuclear moonsault on Lumpy Biscuit and
the crowd are cheering me.
Suddenly, the crowd are holding signs saying
'INTOLERANT OF INTOLERANCE.'
Suddenly, they're chanting a chant whose words are
indecipherable but whose tone isn't. It's adoring. They
adore me. They adore me because I'm good. I'm the
best, even if I don't know why, maybe just because
Lumpy Biscuit is the worst.

Suddenly, and I know I've said suddenly a lot but this
was particularly out of nowhere, Lumpy Biscuit is
saying to me 'YOU MEAN WELL BUT YOU'RE
WEAK. I'M A REALIST. THERE'S NO HIRING
BIAS AGAINST WOMEN IN TECH. THEY JUST
SUCK AT INTERVIEWS.'
Suddenly, I'm saying 'THAT'S BULLSHIT!', and
I sink spears in his side until blood gouts out his mouth
like he's vomiting, endlessly, all over the ring, all over
me, all over the audience, stringy with clots and
bubbly with his breath.
Suddenly, the chants change, or maybe they don't,
maybe the words are the same but the tone is different.
They hate me because I'm bad. I'm the worst, even if
I don't know why, maybe just because Lumpy Biscuit
is the best.

Suddenly, each of my comments is being replied to by
somewhere between thirty and sixty people, and most of
them aren't talking about the article. They're talking
about women being stoned in Saudi Arabia and how
I don't care about that even though I do care about that.

Suddenly, the signs say:

**GRAB HER BY THE
THEY'RE BREAKING WINDOWS NOW
SAME DAY TRAVEL
WHAT ICE CAPS
1488
MURDERED LABOUR MP's**

Suddenly, it's not about me because it was never
about me.
Suddenly, it's about misery and joy, it's yes and no, it's
win and lose, it's us and them.
Suddenly, people everywhere are divided.
Suddenly, people everywhere google 'How did the
polls get it so wrong?'
Suddenly –

IS EVERYTHING OKAY

M *is interrupted by a text from her* MAM.

MAM   **Is everything okay?**

M *asks herself this question. She repeats it aloud to herself over and over. She eventually quietens. Maybe she lies down. Maybe* J, *no longer her wrestling nemesis, helps her.*

M   What are you doing up so early?

MAM   **Couldn't sleep. Have you seen these!!!**

She sends graphic images used by the anti-choice campaign to urge the Irish public to vote 'No' in the Abortion Rights referendum.

M   Yeah, there was loads of that

MAM   **Unbelievable**
Did anyone do anything
The Government

M   Well they let them have posters saying fetuses can yawn and blink at ten weeks

MAM   **Can they not**
?

M   No! I told you the posters were wrong

MAM   **I thought you just meant emotional**
Or manipulative

M   No, wrong like crazy lies that they knew were crazy lies misrepresenting the basic facts about abortion.

MAM   **I didn't know that...**

M   I know
And I'm sorry for going mad at you over the 'casual abortions' thing
But they were deliberately telling crazy lies so we would spend all our time and energy explaining why the crazy lies were crazy lies
And not have any time left to tell the truth
And one of those lies was 'casual abortions'

Like, describe the woman who has a 'casual abortion'
Sorry I'm ranting

MAM   **It is fine I accept your apology**
        !
        I wasn't hurt I was just confused why you were so
        upset

M   Tired more than upset
        But also upset, a man spat on me the day before

MAM   **What**
        !

M   At a march yeah
        So I was upset and tired of being polite to people who
        spit on me
        Of treating it like a debate when they were treating it
        like a war
        And I forgot that that's not everyone
        I forgot that that's not you

MAM   **It is okay**
        !

M   You sure?

MAM   **No**
        Joke
        Yes

M   Oh you got me
        ANYWAY

        How are you?

MAM   **Good, let's have lunch soon**
        !

M   Yeah defo

MAM   **Look after yourself young thing**
        You are Cunt Magic
        !
        MAM

OFFICE 3

M *is in her office, having successfully submitted her article.*
She's looking a little dishevelled.

CARL   **Brilliant.**

M   **Really?**

CARL   **Yeah, little overcomplicated, but it's good.**

M   **Oh. Thanks.**

CARL   **Nice one, sport!**

ALICE   **And, yeah –**
Thanks for the absolutely, y'know –
Great piece –
Really great, and gas, and –
A lot of traffic.
Don't know if you've seen, but –
A lot, like, and –
Oh, just to say we had to edit for length –
Mostly from the stuff about Barthes and politics –
Which is a pity, but you know how things –
How it –
Actually, just all the stuff about Barthes, and politics –
You know how it –
Because it was just a bit –
I mean, you know –
Dense.
I mean, SUPER interesting –
But, still, great work, and –
Eh –
Just, y'know, like –
Gas, like, wrestlers, like, what are they ON, y'know?

M   There's a pause.
We're waiting for me to reply.
We're waiting for me to say 'COOL! FINE!' so we can move on.
And I'm embarrassed, because I find myself explaining, overexplaining, in fact, even though I know they don't and don't have to give a shit.

ALICE   **But, also, y'know –**
There's no –
I suppose –
Absolutely no pressure –
To do that, y'know?
Like, don't kill yourself.
There's absolutely no need for you to kill yourself.
Because if you don't sleep, you –
Like –
Sleep, you silly bitch!
Sorry.
That was –
I shouldn't have –
That was inappropriate.
But I mean it.
Sleep.
Because you're going to die –
If you don't sleep.

DAVE *adds a garbled response to* M*'s article that is vaguely positive in a non-committal way.* M *gives us a wearied look.*

GUARANTEES

Back home.

M   Hey.

J   Hey. I read your article.

M   Really?

J   Yeah. It was great.

M   Thanks. Sure it wrote itself in the end.

J   Did work like it?

M   I think so. But I guess it doesn't really matter that much, does it?

J	Not really. Well not in the grander scheme of things.
M	Maybe we should have called the show that.
J	The Grander Scheme?
M	Yeah. Though it kinda sounds like a farce that might have lots of unfunny dick jokes.
J	Yeah. It's also a crap name.
M	Do you think JERICHO is any better?
J	Eh… I hope so.
M	An excellent vote of confidence.
J	I also hope no one describes it as a farce with unfunny dick jokes.
M	Agreed. Anything else?
J	I hope I remember to buy Shreddies for the breakfast bit tomorrow.
M	And?
J	I hope I pass my driving test next month.
M	I hope you do too.
J	Yeah?
M	I hope to one day own a self-driving car.
J	I hope to one day have two Bernese mutts called Willy and Wonka.
M	I hope there'll be green space where you live to walk them.
J	I hope Dublin developers start building up instead of out.
M	I hope they stop turning clubs into hotels.
J	I hope I never have to vote for Fine Gael again.
M	I hope that the Government introduces a rent-break that keeps my rent at its current level.

J   I hope that one day they'll look at single use plastic the
         way we now look back on asbestos.

M   I hope that if either of us want to have children we can
         afford to.

J   I hope people agree with us enough to forgive how
         earnest we're being.

M   We can't guarantee that, unfortunately.

         At a point early on in the following monologue,
         M directs her attention away from J and towards the
         audience instead.

         We actually can't guarantee any of this.

         Some people think it's all guaranteed.
         The future.
         The universe.
         That that's its arc.
         Towards justice.
         Or away.

         Some people think a post-racial utopia full of people
         with perfect teeth and coffee skin working a five-hour
         week is a dead cert if we just wait long enough and
         make sure the robots aren't evil.

         Some people think it's the opposite, that it's only
         a matter of time until it all ends with a nuclear war
         between Russia and China after brown people topple
         the USA and Europe, which *I* think *they* think would
         be a grave injustice and not just karma.

         But, either way, those people think the universe has
         an arc.
         And that it bends in *a* direction.
         That these things are ultimately guaranteed.
         But when were they guaranteed?
         And who were they guaranteed by?
         And have recent events not made them question those
         guarantees at all?
         How big does a deviation have to be before it isn't
         a deviation?

How bumpy does a road have to be before it isn't
a road?
I suppose it's comforting –
To think that, that there's some impersonal force larger
than, and outside, all of us that gives a shit about what
our actions amount to.
History as a kind of interventionist God without clouds
or a beard –
Or with –
It's not noticeably more or less plausible if History has
a beard.

Or, that's what I believe, anyway.
I don't believe in an arc.
I don't believe in guarantees.
I believe in running as fast as we can to stay on the spot.
And it's impossible to run any*when* but now.
In order to have been running five minutes ago, you
need to have started *more* than five minutes ago.
In order to be running in five minutes, you have to
start now.

OPEN

Christopher Adams & Timothy Allsop

For Adam, David, Gavin, Jack,
Joe, Michael and Sergio

CHRISTOPHER ADAMS

Christopher Adams is a British-American playwright. His play *Tumulus* won an Origins Award for Outstanding New Work at VAULT 2018 and was published in *Plays from VAULT 3*. His full-length plays include *Antigone* (UK tour), *Cooked* (Bread & Roses Theatre) and *Shelter* (Shanghai Repertory Theatre). He has received short-play commissions from the Royal Court Theatre and Theatre503, and his plays *Lynchburg* (2013) and *Haunts* (2015) made the top-forty list for the Bruntwood Prize. He is a US Fulbright Scholar.

TIMOTHY ALLSOP

Timothy Allsop is an actor and writer who trained at the Guildhall School of Music and Drama, where he was a winner of the Michael Bryant Verse-Speaking Award and Lilian Baylis Award. His film and television credits include *The Mummy*, *Captain Phillips* and *Detectorists* (BBC), and his extensive stage work includes *Helen* (Shakespeare's Globe), *Thérèse Raquin* (National Theatre), *Our American Cousin* (Finborough Theatre), *The Picture of Dorian Gray* and *Strangers on a Train* (English Theatre Frankfurt), the lead in *Richard III* (Guildford Shakespeare Company) and *Murder in the Cathedral* (Oxford Playhouse). His novel *The Smog* is published by Amper & Sand.

Open was first performed at VAULT Festival, London, on 23 January 2019, with the following cast:

Christopher Adams
Timothy Allsop

Director	Will Maynard
Co-Designers	Ellie Tranter and Will Maynard
Lighting Designer	Matthew Carnazza
Sound Content	Matt Eaton
Stage Manager	Charlotte Brown
Producers	Chris Davis and Sam Luffman
PR	Stephen Laughton

A Full Disclosure Production in association with Weighed In and Turn of Phrase. The production acknowledges development support from Live Drafts at the Yard Theatre, Hackney Wick.

The writers wish to thank: James Sobol Kelly, Augustina Seymour, Becky Wright, and the members of Playdate.

A Note on the Text

The text in the far-left column is spoken by Tim; the text in the
middle column is spoken by Chris. Text in the right columns is
spoken by a member of the audience or delivered in recorded
voiceover.

Scene One

I'm Tim

   And I'm his husband Chris

We've been together

   Nine years

During that time
Chris has slept with

   Sixty-four people

He knows this
Because Chris keeps a list
He records a name
(If he knows it)
Age
Nationality
Profession
(He always knows what they do)
Any interesting facts

   Number Thirty-Two applied unsuccessfully
   To be on *Great British Bake-Off*

And whether
During their encounter
They fucked him
Or he fucked them

   Tim
   On the other hand
   Does not keep a list
   He has never kept a list
   Partly because before he met me
   He had already slept with
   Forty to fifty men
   He can sometimes recall names

> He never thinks about position
> Because he's almost always a top

The oldest person Chris has slept with is forty-five
The youngest is nineteen

> Tim claims he has never slept with anyone
> Over the age of thirty-five

This is *Open*

> A tale about two guys

One British

> One American

One an actor

> One a writer

(Oh no)

> (No)

(We don't work together often)

> (Probably wouldn't end well)
> (Orton and Halliwell?)

(Whack whack)

> This is a story about
> How we fell in love
> Got civilly partnered

Then married

> Pledged our commitment
> To one another

All the while sleeping with

> Collectively

About one hundred and thirty people
It's a story about

> Sex

It's definitely a story about sex

It's also a story about

Trust and respect

Communication and commitment

As well as
Truth

And lies

We'll start with some truth

Scene Two

This is the first record we have
Of our relationship

CHRIS *has a member of the audience read the following aloud:*

Would you mind reading this aloud?

> Wednesday October 21
> 2009
> At 11:54 p.m.
> IKEA_lampshade
> You have a new message from
> Timothy333
> To read it
> Click the following link
> Remember that you
> Can only use the contact form
> If you've purchased a subscription

Chris debated for
Twenty-seven hours and six minutes
About what to do
In the end though

CHRIS *hands another audience member the following:*

> Dear Subscriber
> Thank you for purchasing
> A one-month Guardian Soulmates
> subscription
> Transactions for the value of:
> £22.45

This is our first
Recorded communication

> October 23
> 12:49 a.m.
> Tim
> Thanks for your message
> My MA is in Chinese literature
> I'm studying at the
> School of Oriental and African Studies
> (SOAS)

Sunday
(Before three)
Would work best for me
Though Monday after seven
Could work too
Chris

> 10:58 a.m.
> Hi there Chris
> Sunday would be lovely
> Maybe a late-morning coffee?
> I also weirdly live between
> Turnpike Lane and Seven Sisters
> So maybe we could head towards
> Crouch End
> On the 41 bus
> And get coffee there?
> Look forward to hearing from you
> Tim

The 41 bus is convenient for me
Which stop?

> Let's meet outside
> Turnpike Lane Tube
> And get the bus from there
> See you then

(*Holding up a coat.*)
The first time I saw Tim
He was wearing this coat

(*Holding up a jumper.*)
Chris was wearing this jumper

> It didn't have patches on it then
> The shoulder wasn't as threadbare

He was wearing these
Brown sort of moccasins
They made his feet look
Sexy

> We went to a café in Crouch End
> I had carrot cake

I had red velvet

     We chatted

He was gentle
Softly spoken
And nervous
He had a chinstrap
It made him look
Amish
And his eyelashes
These long eyelashes
That when he blinked
Made him resemble

     Don't say it

Mr Snuffleupagus

     I don't remember
     Anything we talked about
     I must have had a good time
     But when I went home

When Chris went home
This is how he felt

CHRIS *performs a violent stage action. He is deeply troubled and upset.* TIM *wants to help, but doesn't entirely know how.*

TIM *hands two members of the audience the following conversation.*

     Tuesday 27 October
     Tim
     Lovely spending time with you Sunday
     You're kind
     Interesting to talk to
     And fun to be around
     I'm free Thursday or Friday evening
     If you'd care to go see something together
     Events that come to mind
     English National Opera's production of *Turn of the Screw*
     An Education (film)

Do you like to go dancing?
Anyway
Let me know and we can arrange a time to
meet
I hope you had a good day
Chris

> Hi Chris
> It is a pleasure spending time with
> you too
> I would be very keen to see *Turn of
> the Screw*
> And I do like dancing
> But I wonder whether dancing
> likes me

We went to the opera

> I had a student discount card

It was while riding home on the Tube afterward
That it happened

Well
This is my stop

> Okay

I'd like to see you again

> Okay

I leaned in to kiss him
On the cheek
He was strangely hesitant

TIM *moves in to kiss* CHRIS.

CHRIS *dodges*.

> I knew what he was trying to do
> I didn't know how I felt
> I had never been kissed before
> Certainly not by a man
> In this way
> We were on the Tube

    Surrounded by strangers
    Besides
    Did I really want
    My first kiss
    To be on
    The District line?
    In the end though

TIM *kisses* CHRIS *on the cheek.*

Later that week
Chris told the counsellor he was seeing
A middle-aged Irish man
Whose name he couldn't pronounce
About being kissed by a man
For the first time

His counsellor said

TIM *holds out the script to the audience member:*

    How did that make you feel?

    I felt like a wave
    Not an ocean wave
    One of the math ones
    That has a peak and a trough
    A sine wave
    I felt like a sine wave
    But with the tops cut off

The next time
We were scheduled to see each other
I send Chris this text

Sorry
Going to have to cancel tonight
I've just come down with something

    Oh no
    So sorry to hear that
    I've just bought some vegetables
    I'll come over and make you soup if you like?

CHRIS *takes up a bag and machete and chops veg.*

It's only a little cold
I just feel a bit washed out
Didn't sleep much last night
And I've got this audition next week
Thing is I don't normally get ill

CHRIS *with machete in hand.*

CHRIS *furiously hacks at the vegetables.*

After nine years
He knows that my statement is a lie
An untruth
I am frequently ill

> This will be important later on

But now back to the facts
It is

> 24 November 2009

We are watching

> *John Adams*
> With Paul Giamatti and Laura Linney

It is

> 2 a.m.

You say

> I should go

You could stay here
Sleep over
If you wanted
Just
Sleep

He considers for a while
Then allows me to lead him
Into the bedroom
He takes off his trousers
He climbs into bed
And then rolls away from me

After a moment

> After a moment
> He wraps his arm around me

TIM *wraps his arm around* CHRIS.

Later
When describing this moment
To his counsellor
Chris will say

CHRIS *directs this to the counsellor:*

> That was one of the indicators
> About six months before
> That made me realise
> I was gay
> Not that I found men attractive
> But that I wanted to be held by them

Nothing happened

> Nothing happened that night

The next morning
However

TIM *kisses* CHRIS.

CHRIS *takes off* TIM*'s shirt.*

TIM *takes off* CHRIS*'s shirt.*

The lights fade.

When the lights go back up, CHRIS *is breathing into a paper bag.*

CHRIS *starts to have a panic attack.*

Chris told me
That after we had sex the first time
He went home
And had a panic attack
I was afraid it was my fault
And that he wouldn't want to see me again
But he said it was to do
With his upbringing

And that he would work through it
Because he liked me

CHRIS *hands* TIM *the paper bag.*

TIM *reaches inside the bag and starts to pull out tickets,
receipts, and pieces of paper.*

Over the next several months
We continue to see each other
We go to the cinema

      We go to cheap restaurants

We go to the theatre

      We see all kinds of shows

Jerusalem

      Satyagraha

Henry IV

      The Misanthrope

The Double

      Murder in the Cathedral

TIM *reaches the end of the bag.*

At the bottom of the bag, he pulls out CHRIS*'s American
passport.*

      Tim played Thomas Becket
      It was the first time I had seen him in a show
      I thought
      Thank god
      He's actually a good actor

TIM *holds out* CHRIS*'s passport.*

      Oh
      That

For the record
I hadn't set out
To date an American
Especially not one
Whose visa would expire

31 December 2010

Things were getting serious
In the spring of 2010
I organised a weekend away
At a rustic B&B
In the New Forest
It was as we were
Going out for a walk
That things came to a head

A clunking sound.

Ow
Ow
Fuck

> Oh god
> I'm sorry
> I'm so sorry

He's just dropped a gate latch on my hand

> I've just dropped a gate latch on his hand
> This will be a common feature
> In our relationship
> My hurting Tim
> Inadvertently

Fuck
Why'd you have to do that?

> It was an accident
> Don't cry
> It wasn't that bad
> No seriously you don't need to cry
> What's wrong?

Chris
You should know
I'm starting to
Get attached
If I'm being honest
I love you
And the thought of your leaving

At the end of the year
Makes me feel like shit

> As Tim is saying this
> I feel myself
> Observing
> Myself
> Like my body is standing there
> But my vision is somewhere else
> In our final session
> I had told my counsellor

> I think I have trouble
> Letting myself feel
> Joy

> I tell the counsellor
> The story of Bible camp
> I am thirteen
> There's been a sermon about sex

TIM *has a member of the audience read:*

> If your right hand
> Causes you to sin
> It is better to cut it off
> Than your whole body
> To burn in hell

> Later that night
> After I masturbate
> While thinking about
> The handsome cabin leader
> I go outside
> And I batter my hand with a hammer
> I still have a scar
> On the inside of my thumb

Chris?
Chris have you heard what I said?
I love you

> Hearing Tim say this
> Makes me realise
> Joy is something

That I want for myself
Which is why I tell him

I love you too

And because I'm serious
About us being together
Then I think we should get

Get what?

Civilly partnered

It's important to point out
That in 2010 same-sex marriage
Was not yet legal

Civil partnership was
A new institution
Did it have rules?
It was like marriage
But less defined
Not burdened with
Centuries of tradition
I loved Chris
And Chris needed to stay in the country
And civil partnership allowed for that

Chris will you
Civilly partner me?

Cue Star Trek TNG *music.*

A recorded voice:

Hello and welcome
To the Haringey Civic Centre
Which bears a striking resemblance
To the bridge of the Starship Enterprise
(TNG)
I'm John
Your officiant
We're here today to recognise
Chris and Tim
As they enter this civil partnership
You have chosen to pledge

Your commitment to one another
We witness with hope
That your love and understanding of
Each other will continue to grow

CHRIS *and* TIM *pull out party poppers together.*

Cheers lads!

The sound of cheering.

And that's how we got together
After knowing each other
For barely one year
I was twenty-eight

I was twenty-five

We thought we had
An extended future before us
To explore

Together

A letter lands at their feet.

The mood shifts.

Sound distorts.

What's that?

I think that's the letter.
I never understood why you applied

Honestly
I didn't think I would get it

A recorded voice, as TIM *and* CHRIS *open and look at
the letter.*

24 January 2011
Dear Mr Adams
I am pleased to extend my warmest
Congratulations to you
Upon your selection to receive
A prestigious Fulbright Award
For the 2011–2012 academic year

Your year spent abroad in
Shanghai
China
Will be an opportunity to expose
Your host community to our culture and ideas
While participating in community activities
Sincerely
Mark R Warner
United States Senator

Scene Three

We are in Edinburgh
Because I am in two shows
It's August 2011
Chris's plane to Shanghai
Leaves in a week

> We've just finished having sex
> We have a good sex life
> On average
> We have sex every three days
> I know because
> For the first year
> I keep an Excel spreadsheet
> I'm terrified that if I don't record it
> It never will have happened
> These are the places
> We had sex

CHRIS *hands a list to a member of the audience.*

> Could you read them out?
> With feeling

While the audience reads from the list, TIM *and* CHRIS *make increasingly loud sex noises.*

> *The List*
> On Chris's bed
> On Tim's bed
> In their bed
> In the shower
> In the bathtub
> On their landlord's bed
> On their sofa
> On Chris's parents' sofa
> On their kitchen counter
> In the back garden
> In Tim's dad's house
> In Tim's sister's house
> In Chris's parents' house
> In Chris's grandfather's lakehouse
> In the boat moored by Chris's grandfather's
> lakehouse

CHRIS *and* TIM *scream.*

>Have you got a towel?

No
Just use your T-shirt

>Okay

Sorry

>You alright?

Yeah
Sure
It's just
You're not going to be here
In a week from now
Are you?
And that's sad
Because we won't be able to do this

>You mean sex?

Yeah

>Well I have been thinking

Yes?

>I came across an article
>In the *Australia and New Zealand*
>*Journal of Family Therapy*

You think we need therapy?

>Here
>This section

CHRIS *reads:*

>One of the most interesting findings of our study
>Is that gay male relationships
>Are the only couple type that report equal
>satisfaction
>Whether or not their relationships are sexually open
>or closed

Are you asking
How I feel about open relationships?

> Well
> Look
> You've had sex with other people
> A *lot* of other people
> And I like having sex with you
> I'm not complaining
> It's just that
> You're the only name on my list
> And I wonder what
> Sex with other people would be like

I see

> And as the *Journal* says
> If we were to be
> Open
> Then we
> Statistically
> Have an equal chance of being happy
> As if we weren't in an open relationship

Is that what you want?

> If I'm being honest
> I was scared by what I was proposing
> But somehow it felt like
> The right thing to do
> And besides
> We were civilly partnered
> There were no vows to say
> I hadn't pledged
> That I *wouldn't* sleep with anyone else
> I suppose I was afraid of becoming jealous
> But it wasn't a feeling
> I had ever felt
> Not about Tim
> Because
> Secretly
> Even though we were both
> Deeply in love with each other
> I knew that Tim

> Was fractionally more in love with me
> Than I was with him
>
> How do you feel?

If I'm being honest
Sex with Chris was really hot
He was my type
Boyish looks
Skinny frame
Broad shoulders
And his cheeks
But I have other types too
Shorter
Stockier
Sometimes blond
The thought of being able to sleep
With these people was exciting
Turned me on
But I was also wary
That we might be opening a box
We couldn't easily close

The lights shift.

A forty-five-second clip of YouTube video recordings and comments section with objections to being in open relationships.

While this clip is playing, CHRIS *and* TIM *open a box and discover packing material inside of it. A pair of scissors. Packing tape. And yards and yards of paper.*

As the clip ends, the audio morphs into a breathing sound.

CHRIS *and* TIM *try to shove the materials back into the box. They are mostly successful.*

I'd be okay with that

> You would?

Yeah

> And you don't think our relationship
> Is in trouble?
> We're not trying to compensate for anything?

You still love me
Don't you?

Of course

Then I think we'll be okay

Good
Then we need to create some rules

Scene Four

Recordings:

> Womanshealthmag.com
> Six Rules for Doing the Whole
> Open-Relationship Thing Right
>
> Cosmopolitan
> Ten Things You Must Know Before
> Starting an Open Relationship
>
> HuffPost
> Open Relationships:
> What the Rules Need to Be

Our conversation about rules
Lasts about fifteen minutes
By the end of it
We have decided on the following

One
Always be safe

> Ninety per cent of gay couples
> Have some form of this rule
> We agreed we would always wear condoms
> When having anal sex
> And would make regular visits
> To the sexual health clinic

Two
No sleeping with the same person
More than three times

> Again
> Another common rule
> Designed to preserve
> The specialness of the relationship

Three
No close friends or colleagues

> We quibbled about this one
> Tim has many friends
> Some of whom are very attractive

> Adam?

No

> Will?

Which one?
In any case
The answer's still no

> Tom?

Over my cold
Dead naked body

Four
Don't fall in love

> It's important to point out
> That Tim and my relationship
> As we initially conceived it
> Would be sexually
> Not emotionally
> Open

Five

TIM *whispers in* CHRIS*'s ear.*

> You have got to be kidding
> That's not a rule

It's my rule

> That is a ridiculous rule

If you want me to say yes
You have to agree to this

> I don't understand why this has to be so specific

Because he's exactly your type
And he has a better career than I do

> I feel like if you truly loved me

Bullshit
Say it aloud
I will never sleep with

> I will never sleep with
> Ben Whishaw

Thank you
Is that enough?

> Rule six
> I think we should tell

What do we mean by 'tell'?

> Just tell the other person
> When they sleep with someone
> I'd feel better about knowing

Always?

> It's a common rule
> Ten per cent of couples choose not to
> But I didn't want to be one of them

Fine

> Fine

Fine

> And with that
> We struck our agreement

We were adults

> Having an adult relationship

A *common* adult relationship

> Fifty per cent

Study after study
Shows that nearly

> Fifty per cent

Of gay couples are
In relationships like the one
Chris and I decided upon
There are of course
Other gay people

> The other fifty per cent

Who choose not to be
And that's fine

Completely fine

But there are also
Queer and lesbian couples

About twenty per cent

And straight couples

About five per cent

Who are also in open relationships

That's a lot of people

A lot of humans

A lot of humans
Trying to find a way
To make their relationship work for them
To have a relationship on their own terms
Whether it goes well
Or is
A bit rough

Scene Five

I am in a boxroom
In my dad's partner's house
In Suffolk
Middle-of-nowhere Suffolk
I am supposed to be in China
But instead I am
Unemployed
And convalescing
In March I had visited Chris in Shanghai
But the day I arrived
I felt sick
Twenty-four hours later
I was in a hospital bed
With appendicitis

A week later
I flew back to England
Devastated
Shortly after
This email arrives

CHRIS *hands this email to a member of the audience to read aloud.*

While the email is being read, TIM *opens the box full of construction materials and begins to construct a paper man.*

> Saturday
> April 28
> 2012
>
> Hi babe
> Reading went well last night
> Also
> Been debating whether to email you
> Or tell you over Skype
> But as I'm about to leave for Nanjing
> I figured getting it out there would be best
> Anyway
> I went dancing last night
> Met a guy
> And went back to his place
> He was pleasant and respectful

And I told him beforehand
I wasn't looking for a romantic anything
I have a partner in the UK
Which he was fine with
I think the night
For me
Clarified that
One
I like sex
(Obviously)
And
Two
I miss you
Okay give me a call later if you're around
Lots of love
Chris xxxxxxx

It's the first time
Either of us has slept with someone else
I am feeling alone
Trying to remain calm
Not feel jealous
And trying not to let my imagination
Run away with me

Hey significantly younger man
With lots of money
And a normal-sized nose
Fuck me all night long
And then we can go eat at
Another uber-fashionable
Noodle bar
And go to parties on the Bund
And fall in love
And I'll ditch that sickly English boy

HI LOVE
I WILL SKYPE U AT JUST AFTER 11 A.M.
YOUR TIME SO IF YOU COULD BE FREE THEN
THAT WOULD BE GREAT

Skype sound.

Hello

   Hello?

Hello?
Can you hear me?

   Hello?

Hi
So you slept with someone did you?

   Yes

Who is he?

   I didn't think you wanted to know
   Many details

Did you get his name?

   He was an architect

Where did you meet?

   We met in Shanghai Studio
   The nightclub
   He was standing in a corner
   Smoking

TIM *lights a cigarette.*

   He was shorter than you

TIM *takes on the characteristics of the man as* CHRIS
describes him.

   And a bit older
   Much older actually
   Thirty-seven
   And podgier around the waist
   He reminded me of a goat

TIM *pretends to be a goat, butting* CHRIS *with his head,
increasingly hard.*

   He said

Those jeans look good on you
I haven't seen you here before

> I'm here on a scholarship
> A Fulbright
> It's prestigious

Cool

> And then he put his hand
> In my jean pocket

I'm putting my hand
In your jean pocket
Do you want to come back to mine?

> Okay

Were you safe?

> Of course
> Are you okay?

It's just I'm here in Suffolk
And you know
Recovering
And I thought your email was really blunt

> What did you want me to say?

I wanted you to call me and tell me
Rather than write to me

> How was I supposed to call you?
> It was one in the morning your time

Then you should have waited to tell me
Are you going to see him again?

> Look
> Can you try to be mature about this?

I am trying
I'm just feeling very vulnerable right now
I think the timing of it isn't very good

> I know you're not feeling the best at the moment
> But we talked about this
> We agreed
> We both knew that this
> Could be a thing that would happen

> Like I said in my email
> It was
> Nice
> But it reinforced that
> I love you
> And I want to be with you

Look maybe I need some time
To think it through

Skype call cuts out.

> Hello?
> Hello?
> Tim?
> Tim can you hear me?

TIM *kicks the paper man.*

> Tim
> Tim try to be mature about this
> Tim we need to talk about this
> We need to work through this
> If we don't talk about this
> Then it's going to haunt our relationship

TIM *sets up a shredder.*

May 1
Hi babe
Hooked up with a guy today
Don't remember what his name was
Fucked him for hours

> Tim
> Tim is that true?

It was really really great
Kisses
Tim

> Tim
> Tim what are you doing?

TIM *puts the paper man through a shredder.*

Scene Six

The sound of an airplane.

CHRIS, *with a suitcase.*

>   Hi

Hi
Welcome back

CHRIS *and* TIM *kiss, tentatively.*

They kiss again.

I think we should have another rule

>   And what's that?

Rule seven
No sleeping with someone
Unless we're both in a good place

>   Fine
>   Rule number eight

What's that?

>   Don't be apart
>   For ten months
>   Ever again

Agreed

Scene Seven

Music.

CHRIS *and* TIM *create a home together.*

When Chris returned from China
In the summer of 2012
We moved in together
We lived in
Turnpike Lane

      Bow

Tottenham

      Kilburn

West Hampstead

      We were on an upward trajectory

Chris started working full-time

      Tim got acting work

But that wasn't the only thing
Happening at that time

      The government

The coalition government

      Ah the coalition!

Was starting its discussion
About marriage

      Same-sex marriage

People

      Politicians

Were saying things like

      Opening up marriage
      To same-sex couples
      Would lead to people marrying their toasters

Their pets

> Their houseplants

We end up killing all of our houseplants

> Exactly

Which is why interviews with gay men
At the time
Sounded a lot like this

Clip of interviews with gay male couples. All have been together for decades. Some may have children.

So you see it was awkward
To be open
To talk about openness
Because that wasn't the narrative

> It was counterproductive

Same-sex couples needed to look

> Proper

Committed

> They needed to look

Like straight monogamous couples
Except

> We didn't

We didn't at all

A routine.

With each routine, CHRIS *or* TIM *sets out a miniature paper man.*

> Hi babe
> How was your trip?

Good

Had a guy round
While you were gone

> Oh okay
> Was he nice?

Yep

Another routine.

Hi babe
How was work?

            Meetings all day

Had a guy round
When you were gone

            Oh okay
            Was he nice?

Yep

Another routine.

            Hi babe
            Welcome back from tour

Thanks

            Had a guy round
            While you were away

Oh okay
Was he nice?

            Yep

Had a guy round

            Had a guy round

Had a guy round

            Had a guy round

Had a guy round

            Had a guy round

Had a guy round

            Before we knew it

We felt comfortable

            We each were able to explore
            Things about ourselves

We even discovered
We liked doing things
Together

     Oh
     Hello

Then they start to create a paper man—together.

While they do so, a recording plays:

I am twenty years old. I am a pastry chef.
I first met Christ and Tim because I was living
in the same neighbourhood in London than
them, and we always saw each other on
Grindr. Even though we never talked about it,
you could tell from the start that there was
tension. They were very sexy and caring, hot
and nice. We didn't negotiate anything: it
came all of the sudden one night after playing
some board games while drinking at their
home. And we didn't have sex on the first
encounters: it took like a month or two (and
I liked it a lot, that delay).

We had sex at their house.

It didn't affect at all: they were two guys from
Grindr who wanted to have a drink and talk
with someone. It's so normal where I'm from
in Barcelona. I like them both separate, but
more as a pack, because you can see the
rapport between them and that's appealing.

I think open relationships are the future: I've
been trying to have monogamous
relationships, but the more I try, the more
convinced I am that I will try open
relationships in the future to come.

TIM *and* CHRIS *hug the paper man.*

A feeling of togetherness.

Our rules were working for us
Keeping us safe

Protecting our relationship
Allowing us to have fun

> According to my list
> We were sleeping with a different person
> Once every thirty-four-point-seven days

All was going fine

> Just fine

It was all lovely

> Splendid

Marvellous
Nothing serious threatened our relationship

> Or challenged
> Our feelings for one another
> We were leading liberated gay lives
> In defiance of heteronormative
> Norms

TIM *hands an audience member a small bottle of water.*

Will you take a few sips
And swirl it around your mouth?

TIM *holds out a small plastic cup.*

Now please spit into the cup
Thank you
Can we do that line again?

> What?

'Nothing serious threatened our relationship'

> Oh right
> Nothing serious threatened our relationship
> Or challenged
> Our feelings for one another
> We were leading liberated gay lives
> In defiance of heteronormative

TIM *throws the contents of the cup into* CHRIS*'s face.*

Scene Eight

TIM *hands the following to a member of the audience to read.*

> Crime Reference Number 1700038566
>
> Afternoon Mr Adams
>
> I am writing to you about an incident that happened on the Tube between Finsbury Park and Wood Green where you were subjected to some homophobic abuse and spat at. Please can you let me know if you are happy to proceed with a criminal investigation?

Chris doesn't respond to the officer

> I don't respond

He was riding home
On the Piccadilly Line
Next to him
Was a man

> We met at a bar
> I was taking him home
> I had my hand on his knee
> He reached into his bag
> To show me his copy of
> *Call Me By Your Name*
> And that's when

That's when

Beat.

Chris doesn't respond to the officer

> I don't respond
> I am ashamed
> I think
> If that had been Tim and me
> Being spat on
> And shouted at
> And told we were disgusting
> While a whole Tube carriage looks on
> And does nothing

> Then I would have pursued the case
> I would have had moral righteousness on my side
> But the guy I was with was a hook-up
> So I don't
> Instead I feel like I do
> Back at Bible camp
> I think
> Maybe I deserve it?

> Can we

Can we what?

> Do that line again?

Which line?

> 'Nothing serious'

Sure
Nothing serious threatened our relationship

> Nothing serious threatened our relationship
> Or challenged
> Our feelings for one another
> Sometimes we faced challenges
> Like not knowing how to handle
> Homophobic abuse on the Tube
> But really
> As relationships go
> It was fine
> It was

An iPhone rings.

It continues to ring.

Are you going to answer that?

CHRIS *answers the phone.*

> Hello?
> Hello yes can I call you back?
> I'm kind of in the middle of something

CHRIS *falls silent.*

CHRIS *ends the call.*

What?

> Um
> That was the STI clinic
> Apparently I have
> Um

What?

> Gonorrhoea
> In my throat
> I need to go in for treatment
> You should too

Are you kidding me?

> It's not a big deal
> Lots of people
> Straight as well as gay
> Get STIs
> It's easily treatable
> Just swallow these pills
> And bend over and take the shot

Ow

> Now where were we?

Nothing serious

> Nothing serious threatened our relationship
> Or challenged our feelings for one another
> Nothing

Chris

> What?

I think we should go to the clinic

> We don't need to go to the clinic

We didn't wear condoms

> We agreed
> In this instance
> It would be okay
> Not to wear condoms

We fucked him
Without wearing condoms

>Because his profile said
>He's on PrEP

People lie all the time
On their profiles

>He seemed trustworthy
>He was an accountant

I can't believe you talked me into it

>You didn't take much convincing

I was drunk

>Didn't it feel good?

That's not the point
We need to go to the clinic
Right
Now

>I have to go to work

You shouldn't've put us
In this situation
We're going to the clinic

>Fine we'll go to the clinic

Fine

>Fine

Fine

>We went to the clinic
>It was fine
>As I was saying

Nothing serious

>Nothing serious threatened our relationship

Or challenged our feelings for one another

>Maybe sometimes we went
>Further than we intended

But we were able to be honest
About our actions

And trust each other implicitly

If anything
Being open made us more communicative

More subtly attuned to
The other person's needs and desires

A WhatsApp message sounds in the audience.

Ahem
More subtly attuned to the other person's needs and desires

Another WhatsApp message sound.

And another.

Oh for goodness' sake

CHRIS *investigates.*

He shines a torch around the audience, trying to find the culprit.

A paper man in the audience.

CHRIS *goes to the paper man.*

The paper man has a phone.

Another WhatsApp message sound.

Tim?

CHRIS *looks at the phone.*

Another WhatsApp message sound.

Tim?
Who's Peter?

An interrogation spotlight.

It happened while we were living
In West Hampstead
I was between acting jobs
Which meant I had
Time to waste on Grindr
I messaged a guy
Peter

He looked a lot like Chris
But blond
And Australian
More tanned
And with a tattoo of an aeroplane on his foot
We hooked up a couple of times
And I was going to tell Chris about it
But something was different about this

The thing is
When Chris and I have sex
I am a top
And Chris is a bottom

But with Peter
He was more

I let him top me
And it was good
It felt really good
Because it's often
Impossible for me to feel relaxed enough
And I could do things sexually
That Chris and I
Couldn't do with one another
Because we'd find it too funny
Or we'd be distracted by thoughts
Of the shopping we needed to organise
Or buying birthday presents for my mother-in-law
I mean
That was the whole point of sleeping with other people
Wasn't it?
That it wasn't domestic

And I was going to tell Chris
But somehow
I felt dirty talking about it
Every time I said
'Had a guy round'
I felt
A stab of
Shame
But also

Resentment
That I couldn't have
Something to myself

>   Tim
>   Who is Peter?

A guy

>   Did you sleep with him?

Yes

>   We're supposed to tell each other
>   Why didn't you?

A day passed
And then it seemed weird
To bring it up

>   But now it's really weird
>   So what did you do?

Why do you always need to know the details?

>   Because you didn't tell me
>   And I'm concerned
>   Did you jerk off?
>   Did you fuck him?

Actually
He fucked me

>   I didn't know
>   That was something you were in to

Neither did I really
I suppose
That's why I didn't bring it up
I promise you
I've told you about everyone else

>   If it's easier for another guy to fuck you
>   Then that's how it is

Is this going to threaten our relationship?

>   Nothing serious is going to threaten our relationship

It's our relationship

       We're responsible for each other

We're responsible *to* each other

       Just the two of us

It doesn't challenge *our* feelings

       It doesn't challenge how *we* feel

This is about us

       About how we as a couple

The sound of a radio being tuned.

CHRIS *and* TIM *are perplexed.*

A voice enters the space.

          Well the first time that I slept with both of you at the same time I'd never had that experience outside of drugs. It's a strange feeling to be the person that is the new thing introduced into the sexual situation. So I think it would be some people's fantasy to be like *the* exciting new element right? But I think I was quite nervous about it, really unsure of where I was in myself and I find it quite difficult because I was aware that it was what you both wanted. And – I don't know how to say – I felt – it didn't feel like a level playing field. I was in your home. Here's two people who live with each other, who have sex with each other. I was different. I think what happened was, now that I'm saying it out loud and given the opportunity to reflect on it, I think that because I was probably feeling quite vulnerable about sex, I felt really hyper-aware of feeling a bit like a toy. It was fun. I enjoyed it. But you'll notice that like I left straight away afterward – I felt really uncomfortable. Directly after that I was always scared about coming over for dinner, because I didn't know what would be expected.

Okay so maybe

    Maybe possibly

Maybe possibly we hadn't considered
The effect our relationship had
On other people

    The power we have as a couple

Our needs

    Our desires

Playing with men

    Other humans

As if they were
Toys to be pulled out of a box
Whenever we needed them

    Partly it's a defensive mechanism

Transactions are easier

    Though some lovers have become friends
    It's usually after we've become post-sexual

Blending sex and friendship
Can be dangerous territory

    We don't want anything
    To threaten our relationship

I love Chris

    I love Tim
    Maybe Tim loves me a little bit more
    Teeny bit more than I love him

A beautiful thing

    There can be no one else

I trust him implicitly

    No one serious

I have complete faith

    Maybe my eyes can wander

That nothing will threaten us

> But my heart will always be true
> Always be faithful

But

There is a loud groan from offstage.

TIM *looks concerned and exits.*

> I love Tim so much

TIM *returns pulling something large.*

> Of course I do
> I mean he was the first person
> I went on a date with

He struggles with it.

> The first person I kissed
> The first person I slept with
> We have so much *history*

It is a long paper arm attached to a long paper body.

> So what if occasionally I wonder
> What it would be like
> To have found someone else first
> Someone with an interest say
> In New York avant garde theatre
> Who directed shows at The Public?

He carries on the body of a monster paper man, ten feet high.

> Or someone cute and charming
> And I don't know why I am so in to him
> Other than that he's unbelievably cute and charming
> And we could go on holiday together
> And I can stare at his incredibly cute ass

It groans.

> Or perhaps someone older
> An academic
> A prize-winning academic
> Who speaks French
> Better yet

> *Is* French
> What would life be like
> With that person?

Chris can you help me with this?
I'm kind of drowning here

> > Can you be careful?
> > You're knocking things over
> >
> > Would a French academic
> > Constantly knock things over?

Would you pay attention
To what's going on
Look at the monster in our house

> > I don't know what you're talking about
> > I think you've gone crazy
> > You know you're a very anxious person
> >
> > I bet the French academic
> > Isn't an anxious person
> > In fact I'll text him to ask if he is
> > He gave me his number at a conference

Chris the monster
In our house
Is making me feel uncomfortable

> > Monster?
> > There is no monster
> >
> > Over drinks
> > The French academic quotes Derrida about monsters

It's going to eat you

> > Of course it's not going to eat me
> > You always jump to conclusions
> > Everything is under control
> >
> > Speaking of eating
> > I wonder what kind of food
> > The French academic likes?
> > I bet he likes cheese
> > Tim doesn't digest cheese very well

> I'll find out
> Because he's asked me out to dinner

The giant paper man starts to attack CHRIS.

Chris it's starting to eat you

> Nothing is wrong

The man starts to subsume CHRIS.

Chris this is ridiculous
We can't go on like this
I think you're in denial
I think you're really in to this guy

CHRIS *is lost in the paper man.*

> Well you know how it is
> I prefer to get to know a guy
> Before I sleep with him
> I'm not like you
> Fuck and go

But you keep meeting him for drinks
And dinner
And you text him all the time
Turning your phone away

The sound of digesting.

TIM *grabs the paper man.*

No this is too much
I'm going to take him away

> You can't do that
> You have no right to do that

CHRIS *grabs the other end of the paper man.*

They get into a tug of war.

> Get off him

No
You let go

> No
> You let go

No

     Let go

No

The struggle climaxes with the paper man being torn.

     Look what you've done to him
     You've broken him
     All I wanted was to be close
     To him
     I loved listening to his voice
     His face
     I loved being around him
     I loved
     I

You loved him

Beat.

     I did

Beat.

Nothing serious threatened our relationship
Or challenged our feelings for one another

     Stop
     Don't throw it in my face

What?
Pretend like it doesn't hurt
For you to have feelings
For someone else
To pretend to be okay
While you lose yourself
In someone else
I feel like you take me for granted
That I'm just a housekeeper
Your cook
You're being very selfish

     Could you please
     Try to have some compassion?
     It's very hard when

> Someone breaks your heart
> And it's embarrassing and
> Shameful
> I feel ashamed
> I don't want to admit
> To have to admit to someone
> To have to admit to you
> That I'm hurt
> And I know it's my fault
> And I know I don't deserve to be loved
> And I feel
> So
> Completely
> Ashamed

To audience.

And that made me stop
Because that word
Shame
We had both felt it
So many times

> Tim felt it every time
> He had to tell me
> He had slept with another guy

Chris felt it when he
Didn't think he deserved to have
His attack investigated
By the police

> Tim felt it after he
> Had condomless sex

Chris felt shame
Every time he went for a drink with a guy
Before going home with him
What if they ran into someone they knew?
How would he be explained?

We both felt it
Every time we had to find words
To describe the people we were with

This is my *friend*?

Lover?

Companion?

Squeeze?

Friend with benefit?

English doesn't have
Satisfactory words to describe
The fine web of relationships
That exist for gay men

This is a guy I'm going to sleep with
And we'll never see each other again
But the moments that we're together
Are meaningful

This is a guy I slept with a few times
And now we're post-sexual
And really good friends
But still flirt outrageously

This is the guy I saw repeatedly
Because of our shared foot fetish
But he also gave us a lovely set of bedsheets
And set of kitchen spoons
When we moved into our new flat

More importantly
English lacks words for the *feelings*
The emotional landscape
These relationships cause us to experience

Chris is jealous of another guy
Who is seeing someone else
Am I jealous of his jealousy?

Tim has a flippant approach
To hook-ups
Which sometimes I envy

Chris falls in love
With someone else
Which upsets me
But at the same time
I see that he's hurt

And I see that
At the root of his hurt
Is shame

Chris

> Yes Tim?

I can't pretend it's not hard
To hear that you have feelings
For another guy
And I don't like feeling jealous
And maybe that's not your fault
Maybe I can choose not to be jealous
Or maybe I can feel jealous
And that's okay
Maybe I need to talk it out
I suppose even though we're gay men
We're still men
When I think about my dad
And his dad
They never expressed their feelings
And never taught me to express mine
So I want to tell you
That I love you
And I don't want you to feel ashamed
About how you feel toward this other guy
Or ashamed to tell me
How you feel about him
The only way we're going to get through this
Is to be open with one another
And not allow the outside world
To dictate how we feel
Or how we should behave

> I feel like I've spent half my life
> Trying to make things easier for
> Other people
> I don't want to feel
> Shameful about the kind
> Of relationship we've built

Then we're okay?

> We're okay

So in some ways
It's true

> Nothing serious threatened our relationship
> Or challenged our

Commitment

> Commitment for one another

We're not saying that it's not
Hard work
Or that it's free of consequences

> We're not saying that it's for everyone

Or that we'll always choose
To be in this form of relationship

> But like everyone else
> We're searching for
> An authentic way to achieve

Connection

> Pleasure

Joy

> And while our relationship
> Shares certain parts of ourselves
> There are things that have happened
> Such as

Lying in bed together and holding each other
Over the Christmas when Chris's grandpa is
Dying in the next room

> Watching entire box sets together

Watching terrible plays together

> Making an effort
> With each other's families

That are private
That aren't open
There are even some things
That not even you can know

Scene Nine

And so we come to the 26 of June 2015
It is a Sunday afternoon
We are on Hampstead Heath

> I have just checked my phone
> The United States Supreme Court
> Has legalised same-sex marriage across the nation

>> The history of marriage is one of both
>> continuity and change. That institution –
>> even as confined to opposite-sex relations –
>> has evolved over time.

> I suggest we head up to the tumulus
> Shall we go up here?

Sure

> I walk us around three times
> Nervous
> Working up the courage

CHRIS *turns to* TIM.

> I think about everything
> That happened to bring me
> To this point
> I think about Bible camp
> I think about coming out to my parents
> I think about seeing a counsellor
> I think about moving across an ocean
> So that I can be who I am
> But I also think about
> Love and commitment
> And having those recognised
> On my own terms

> So I turn to Tim and say

> Will you marry me?

I can think of all the terrible things
That marriage means
What it has meant over the years

How marriage has been used
To deny rights to all kinds of loving relationships

How as gay men we don't have to
Model that kind of relationship

But how now
Marriage is no longer a closed institution

It's an open one

Open to change

Perhaps even more radical change
Than it is aware of

I think about all the people I've slept with

All the people we will sleep with

And imagine them standing there
Alongside us

And I think
This is Chris

And this is Tim

So I answer

Yes
Yes I will

THROWN

Jodi Gray

*For Jill
of course*

JODI GRAY

Jodi Gray is a playwright and screenwriter. She is Associate
Artist with Vanner Collective and Living Record. She works
extensively with drama schools and community theatre groups.
Plays include *Thrown* (Living Record at Edinburgh Festival
Fringe 2018, winner of the Brighton Fringe Award for
Excellence; VAULT Festival 2019); *Big Bad* (VAULT Festival
2018, winner of the Origins Award for Outstanding New Work;
London Horror Festival at the Old Red Lion, London); *Peep*
(Bewley's Theatre Café, Dublin, February 2018, published by
Nick Hern Books); *Affection*, *hookup*, *You Could Move*, *Reach
Out and Touch Me*, *The Front Room* and *SSA* (all Outbox
Theatre, in London and on tour). Short plays include
Finale (Caravan Shorts); *This Girl* (Bold Tendencies); *Broken
Meats* (Salt at Southwark Playhouse); *Quirks* (Southwark
Playhouse); *He's Not There*, *Peep*, *Tasty* and *Rime* (Miniaturists
at Arcola Theatre). She has also written the short films *Broken
Meats* (dir. Sam Phillips); and *Sidetracked* (dir. Freddie Hall;
nominated for Best Writer at Underwire Festival 2015).

Author Acknowledgements

Special thanks and love from me to Jill and Ross for trusting
and inspiring me with this incredible idea, and to Jess and Chris
for making it all happen so beautifully.

J.G.

LIVING RECORD PRODUCTIONS

Living Record Productions is a theatre company founded by Ross Drury and Jill Rutland. Alongside their binaural theatrical productions they are also creating an online archive of collected testimony called 'The Record of Living' – true stories from the end of childhood retold and relived from people all over the country. These interviews, which inspire the production, are available to watch on the company's YouTube Channel: www.youtube.com/LivingRecordProductions

SPUN GLASS THEATRE

Spun Glass Theatre is a theatre production company who create partnerships with independent artists and companies to combine their signature ethos of artist-led audience development, fundraising and project management with each artist's vision and form, creating more space for great art to be made.

'The dimensionality of care will ultimately be interpreted in terms of the three temporal dimensions: past (thrownness/ disposedness), future (projection/understanding), and present (fallen-ness/fascination).'

Michael Wheeler, *'Martin Heidegger'*,
Stanford Encyclopedia of Philosophy

326

Acknowledgements

Firstly, thanks to Christine, Diane, Dot, and all the women who
let us use their truths and turn them into poetry. We are forever
grateful for your honesty and wicked humour.

Thanks also to Richard Warburton, Ivan Mack and everyone
who makes Theatre in the Mill, Bradford, work so brilliantly for
companies in need of space, time, and a bit of northern soul.

Thanks to Arts Council England for your ongoing support,
and to The Spire, James Turnbull, Simon Magnus, Alex Levene
and everyone at The Place Theatre, Bedford, Age UK, Hop 50+,
HM Prison Bedford and the Retired Caribbean Nurses
Association.

And finally, thanks to Steve Rutland, Heather Marshall, Luke
Barton and Melissa Campbell for your shoulders to cry on,
creativity to hang on, and beds to sleep in.

Thrown premiered at Big Belly at the Underbelly at the Edinburgh Festival Fringe, on 5 August 2018, produced by Living Record Productions. The cast was as follows:

DR CONSTANCE ELLIS   Jill Rutland

Director   Ross Drury
Sound Designer   Chris Drohan
Producer   Jessica Cheetham
                            for Spun Glass Theatre

A work-in-progress version of *Thrown* was previewed at Theatre in the Mill, Bradford, on 16 June 2018.

The play transferred to Network Theatre, London, as part of VAULT Festival, on 6 March 2019, with the following addition to crew:

Lighting Designer   Lewis Fowler

Character

DR CONSTANCE ELLIS

Notes on Text

Left-aligned italicised text is stage directions.

Left-aligned non-italicised text is live speech.

Centred italicised text is recorded speech, or echoes from elsewhere.

An ellipses (...) indicates a beat or pause.

The 'breaks' in the play (— — —) indicate a shift in time or place – Constance recording later, or stories happening outside of her particular space.

In the original production, we used a binaural microphone shaped like a human head and the audience were wearing wireless headphones. But Constance could be using any kind of recording equipment, and headphones are not vital – although some kind of soundscape is.

CONSTANCE *is there in the space as the audience enters. Possibly there's a chair for her, some props for her – as if she's in an attic containing things from the span of a life. She's checking her recording equipment.*

She takes a moment.

Eventually –

Hello. I'm Constance Ellis. You know that because –

You're.

…

I'm not sure who I'm talking to. Should I say 'I' or 'You'?

Difficult to know whether you'll recognise me. Recognise yourself.

Would it be easier if I say 'we'?

Done this so many times with other people. Can't work out how we got them to be so forthcoming now, how they found it so easy to talk and to. Um.

Is this thing on?

Is this thing on?

I'm making a – record, recording. I'm – I want you to hear my voice, in case it helps you remember. I'm assuming that you want to – that you would rather have some – memories, some something to hang yourself on.

…

I'm a doctor. You were a doctor. You are a doctor. You also, um, *will be* a doctor, actually, I –

I suppose it'll get confusing if I keep doing that. Which is – you know – the opposite of what I'm. We're aiming for something like clarity here, aren't we.

...

We were a psychologist. Specialising in children, childhood, so more specifically a child psychologist – for clarity's sake. 'Doctor' being the more general –

Fuck it.

I'll start again.

...

Although, ha, if you're struggling to remember me, you – then this will remind you what an unsure sort of person I am. You will be feeling unsure of yourself now as you listen to this but I want to remind you that you have always been that way. This way, the way I am.

I can't hear anything –

'Temporary', the husband called me once, but I took it – actually – as a compliment. Cuz when they tried to pin me – box me and press the lid down, make me into a more definite sort of person, I would fight. Could be that's why you're so insubstantial now. Maybe I did this to you.

I won't start again.

Not just yet.

...

I want to tell you I want you to know that nothing bad is going to happen to you. I'm here, I'm here, I've always been here with you and I'll always be there with you, even when you think you've lost me I'll be here. Or there. Or.

You can trust me. Is what I mean.

You could maybe have your eyes closed, if you like. Keep them closed. Maybe it will make more sense with your eyes closed.

But you can see me now, if you look. If you listen you can hear me.

Can you hear me?

Can you see?

I want you to do it all in your own time. It's important, I think, for you to do this in your own time.

Listen:

I'm here. Breath in, and breathe out. We're – here. Listening·to each other still. Still beating heart and breathing lungs and believing believing – believing me.

…

I hope that you can believe me now.

I was six.

I was eight, maybe.

I was here.

I was twenty-five.

Do you remember when we were –

I'll start again.

— — —

Do you remember at dinner parties when they would say – they'd say something like –

'Oh, not *really* a doctor then – '

As if the mind weren't as important as the body, as if what we were doing was less – surgical. Less precise. And then as if a child's mind was somehow less important again. But we'd be thinking about all the cuts and the breaks and the scars we'd seen in the mind of a child and we'd take in a breath to say –

…

But it never came out, did it. Coward. And those men who said that, naval-gazing at their own hands, marvelling at their life-giving digits. Couldn't believe anything could be as important as them. Always the men, wasn't it, always the fucking surgeons. Those fucking Bastards. Haha.

Conveniently forgetting about all the life us women have given over the years – as well as all the times they'd totally fucked it and taken life instead.

…

I wanted my own children, I think. Not desperately, not even instinctively, but there, you know, was a want there, for a while.

There were friends' babies – some of them well and some of them, unwell – and, how could I do that? Here is something so pure and me knowing the whole world was out there waiting to gobble them up.

How did we know that?

But anyway it wasn't to be and didn't happen and didn't happen and the husband lost faith in me, and I lost the will to take the protective covering off another human being. It felt cruel, somehow, knowing what I know.

And so it ended, and finally he went, and I felt.

Nothing.

That world is not for us.

And what did we know anyway?

— — —

From eighteen to twenty-one I –

I turned twenty-three on an autumn –

Twenty-five.

The sky to me is curved.

What's happening?

– what happened to me?

(*Re: recording equipment.*) I'm hoping that you will recall Frank here. He was our coworker. Never talked much but a very good listener. Haha. Not great at eye contact either but then neither was I, so.

I made him because, we – we, well, were mining for memories, weren't we? We wanted to find out how a person – how we as humans create a satisfying life story from – from these shards of – of, of, *conscious–*, or – no, not. Ha. Sorry, the word escapes [me].

…

So, we decided, we would try to understand childhood better by coming at it from the other end of life – we wanted to extract traumatic childhood incidents from ancient women, and then see what happened in between – child to adult to old age. We believed we could sift through these women's lives for clues and correlations. If *A* happens to the child, does it follow that *B* happens to the adult, or that they become a total *C*?

We talked to women because women, for the most part, are more practised at talking about themselves. More excited about being listened to. Plus, they live longer, so we could look at a bigger span of years. And that's just maths.

You can imagine us now: strutting and swaggering in to talk to them armed with our rude youth, and Frank. This is those who could recall themselves with any detail, of course. If they had lost their minds along the way, then what use were they to us, poor old dears?

Ruthless.

…

So anyway, we surmised, he – Frank – meant we could record and – with the headphones we could make them listen, to sounds or songs or words that would – we hoped would create a world in their heads and work something loose without us having to say too much.

We would ask them only –

'When did you know you were no longer a child?'

– and they would have such –

Oh you don't wanna hear my story –

I don't know if I've got anything very interesting –

You don't want to talk to me.

But in the end they would come up with something so –
specific. Quite cheerfully launching into stories about bombs
and death and high heels. And, in the end, for the most part,
they found it cathartic. To tell us these tales and work out their
relevance, the thread running through the life which binds the
story together.

What was our story?

Just ignore that.

Why did we never ask?

It's nothing.

Why won't you listen to her?

…

We did not, it's important to note at this stage, believe that *we*
would ever get old. We still had an idea that, somehow, at some
point, we would be taken aside and told not to worry –

'*Of course* it was all just an elaborate test. And you passed!
Congratulations. Now, what age would you like to be? Because
you can stay just that age forever. Old age will never happen to
you.'

But – look at you now.

So – if that's what you remember. If when you look in the
mirror now you see an ancient old woman and you think for a
moment that her stories are yours –

Please don't be too angry.

It will never happen to you.

Even though we'll probably be fucking furious about it.

…

Ha. I've lost my thread now.

— — —

Ta-dah!

I was – a clown. I was a clown, wasn't I? That's right. In the end I become a clown.

Black – satin – dinner suit. Oh yes. Bow tie. A waistcoat like riches, gold sequins and shine. Top hat – oh yes – with a Big, White, Feather. Dance shoes – of course, for dancing, forever dancing now. And – big red nose. Look at me go.

I always thought I'd be a glamour girl, but, no – clown's more me. Don't you think?

Stop making me laugh, it hurts!

I like to entertain, see, I liked to delight to distract, to –

I was eleven. My mother. She was fierce she and soft, she was – laugh like bubble gunshots like pepper like bouncing off the walls. That's the first thing I notice, the first time I know something's not all right, cuz the laughing goes. So I'm scared then cuz I loved that laugh, was life, that laugh, was she.

I would dance for her, even though I'm not a good – clown-dance for her, make her laugh, pull laughs from her mouth and. She lying in bed – the lounge now her bedroom because the stairs had become –

She couldn't move couldn't spin or waltz or go upstairs but we – my father, such a handsome, such a beautiful dancer. We would dance for her we would –

It hurts.

I was eleven, she died.

Her heart was like a boot.

– they said and I thought they must be talking about someone else's heart – not hers, like a boot. Not she.

And he my father would go out every night go out and go out dancing every night and not me because still just a girl but he.

You're beautiful. Look at you.

Every night he'd dance away.

And me alone now.

And he alone too, I thought. He's alone just like I'm alone now. So he dances.

And I clown.

I was eleven. When I felt loneliness. Saw it in him and saw its twin in me, I think – that was –

That was when I first –

…

…

Was that me?

No. That was Christine. One of our old women.

We're a doctor aren't we, weren't we, will we not be a doctor?

That's right.

That's what you said before –

Yes. Don't worry.

I wasn't a clown at all.

Very good.

…

I mean, that's not even my bloody accent.

— — —

The sky to me –

Seven years.

I'm thirty-two.

Three months.

Eleven.

Five.

Three days.

An hour.

I want to know – I've wondered – would you want to know how many days, if you were me? How many – And if you knew how many days, would you count them? Would you count them down to the knowing, or would you try to forget.

Like childhood, isn't it. Ironically. That arsehole Catch-22 we've been bothering away at all our lives. If you know your childhood will end, then you've already lost it. Or at least the most important part of it.

Do you remember – the boy with the long hair, he asked us –

'Do I have to grow up?'

And he was genuinely terrified, wasn't he! He said it looked like a load of poo – which of course it was, and is, and will be. And we didn't have the heart to tell him that asking that question meant he was already halfway there.

…

I'm recording this for selfish reasons because I'm frightened. I'm afraid that if you forget me, I will disappear. If the bits of me go from you – Because where would I be then? Poor Old Dear. That's where.

Thing is, we always felt safe before in the folds of the brain. But there's no safety for me in those soft pink ripples any more. Because yours are unfurling and letting me go and I will be –

My mind is playing tricks on me already. I am somehow already flimsier, already dispersing, since they told me. Since our 'diagnosis', as if the words, like a trigger – . Oh, but how wonderful it must be to be able to *diagnose*, to give an answer to a question rather than always always searching searching –

Though they weren't able to say exactly how long it will be before you forget the story of me. Which means there is still a question – ha!

But only you can answer it.

…

Did you hear it?

When it went, when I started to go, when you went from yourself –

Just so I can listen out for it.

I want to know what sound it makes.

— — —

Look at me, I'm fifteen.

I still remember the way I felt –

The way it feels I remember –

How soft my skin –

How bright the eyes –

How fast the feet how fleet how fantastic –

I'm sixteen.

I am seventeen.

I'm fifteen.

A breath – in and out.

I remember being being being fifteen.

It was a choice I made – to grow up.

I remember when I was fifteen – there was a time when I was.

On the outside I look, but on the inside I'm.

There's this exhilaration, this knowing that I have changed. Or something some part of me has changed. Inwardly, on the inside, everything is different, and it is –

But on the outside I am still – childhood I am still.

But inside I am everything.

Okay – borrowed clothes and lipstick and hair piled up to here, and shoes like tottering shoes so I look like I feel like I look.

So – the outsides of me matched the insides of me so I feel like I look like I feel.

They aren't fooled, of course, I will find out later. The real grown-ups, the ones who don't need to pretend, they aren't fooled. But I fool myself and – fake it till you make it, they say that, don't they. I rehearse. And it works.

So. I fake my way into the cinema on legs in heels, and clothes not mine and hair up there and lips on fire and.

There was a time when I was fifteen. When I told the world – I'm here. Just look. Look at me go.

…

That wasn't me either.

No. It wasn't. Well done. That's Diane.

But it wasn't us.

As if we were ever that sure of ourselves.

I'm tired.

Me too.

— — —

The husband used to say that I wasn't held enough when I was small. By way of explanation, explaining me to myself in a way, which – you know, really seems like a horrible thing to say to someone actually doesn't it. I said –

'I don't feel the need to explain myself, why do you?'

But he just laughed and held me tighter as if he'd never stop as if he could send the holding back in time to the small version of me. But neither small me or adult me could breathe then and we'd wriggle and elbow until he'd have to let me go. Until he stopped even trying.

…

I wonder if you know that I'm not being fair to you. I'm asking you to puzzle yourself back together from these pieces I'm giving you, but maybe you already know there are pieces missing. How are you supposed to make yourself out so covered in holes?

So, then – who am I really doing this for?

Me?

Or you?

Or her.

…

The smaller self.

The little upside-down one who was the starting of us.

…

I'm looking around now and packing up and wondering where her toys went. Which is weird. We must have had toys. We must have had games and best friends and running so fast down hills our bodies overtook our legs and we helter-skeltered on the grass and then got up and just kept running.

…

You should have told me this already.

I should have told you what?

You have to go back.

Why?

'Other children have parents who' –

…

Go on!

Other children they have parents who save their toys and their drawings and their first-step stories.

And we didn't have parents.

– not birth parents, not anyone we can remember as having been the ones who made us.

So – tell me.

…

There was a care home until we were six. And then other
people's homes after that. And those people repackaged the toys
after we had gone for the new girls and boys that came when we
went. Ebb and flow.

Always left or always leaving and helpless in the waves of it,
I thought, why hold on to anything? Even the idea of myself,
my – self, why am I holding on now? We knew never to take
things for granted. Anyone could be taken away, anything, if we
could be taken away –

Just maths.

…

I keep thinking I could have done something before now that
would have made things easier for you. If we did have children,
now, and they could look after you. If I'd married one of the
lovers or even stayed married the first time –

Though he's dead now. Not sure how much good that would do
you, being married to a dead man, buried now and mulched –
what will he be able to tell you about yourself that I can't?

Yeah, well admittedly maybe some outside perspective would
be useful. But I don't have those details, do I, those bits of
myself that someone else might have noticed or cherished. But
let's not kid ourselves we were cherished, really. Or that we
even knew how to be.

So much about me that's forgotten now. Only a little of me
really for you to forget so why am I still fucking *doing this*?

…

Is she something you want to remember?

>   *That's where we came from. We both grew out of her.*

Hey – can you talk to her where you are? The small one. I don't
know – I don't know why it makes me feel better now to
imagine that you're somewhere together.

It's only –

I can't hear her.

What's she saying?

Tell her –

…

I miss –

— — —

I was nine.

I don't remember being scared, or.

I was eight.

Eleven or around –

*Well I mean it was just the way things were, it was just life,
you're not scared of –*

We were six.

I'm nine.

Oh. Nine? I was.

*We had to sleep in the crypt under the church. Yes.
So, we would – we would hear the siren, we would go
quickly to the church. But it was only a game, we thought,
we weren't afraid – us little ghosts in moonlit nightdresses,
slipping through the graveyard, shamelessly mocking the
greedy dead, quite blithely alive.*

Come on, and quickly now.

*And under the ground, under the church, laying down
to sleep on the tombstones, hundreds and hundreds –
the tombs stretching all away into the dark.*

If I should die before I wake –

*Here we are, us warm bodies, pretending to sleep
through the shudder and slip of bombs on the earth above
and – my tomb has the Lord's Prayer on it so I trace the
words with my fingers and wonder how much further down
we'd have to go to get to Hell.*

All the lights go out and I have my answer.

A moment, just breath.

> *In the morning. Up the stairs from the crypt to the church*
> *to the graveyard. From the fat dark to the fine light*
> *to the deafening sun.*

> *But there are ghosts here still, even without the moon.*
> *Row upon row of white sheets upon bodies, new dead*
> *upon old dead upon new, and the new just as greedy*
> *as the old. They must know, they must be able to smell*
> *to taste all the life I have in me now.*

> *The rest of my life I have in me.*

> *And finally afraid.*

NO.

That's. Not. Me.

> *I know it's not – you have to calm down. You're upsetting*
> *yourself.*

I'm not an old woman, I didn't survive the Blitz I didn't even
know my mother.

> *No. I know.*

> *I know.*

Why are you making me listen to this?

> *I don't know. I'm trying to help.*

It's not helping it's confusing. I feel mad.

> *You're not mad.*

What am I then?

…

You're –

— — —

What happened to us?

I don't remember.

Liar. Coward.

Ha – yes. That's true.

…

There must have been a time when we didn't think we would ever stop running.

Most you can do to stand now, probably.

Heaving yourself up with a creak and a moan from the chair to snatch the last biscuit and drop of tea from the other old women with their claws and their veins and their total inevitability.

I am fucking furious about it. For the record.

…

Other women, they – don't they have parents, aren't there children to keep a record of their lives so they don't forget who they are when their minds go to shit.

Unfortunately we have to make do with.

With me.

I'm sorry I didn't believe –

Like you've always had to make do with me.

…

But – we have our old ladies, don't we. The comfort that their rich tales of lost childhood and crumbled lives will always offer when weighed against our – only ever incidental self.

No offence.

…

What we never really understood is that we shouldn't have recorded what they remembered. We should have recorded what was forgot. It's in those gaps where the life lives.

Could be you'd rather forget.

Can't work out if I'm going forwards or backwards now.

We have to go –

I mean, when I become ancient you and you forget me and then you become like a child again, will the child in turn forget you and turn into me? And will it happen again and over and – all of us pretending we don't know what comes next?

What age will you choose?

When they take you aside and ask you –

Now, what age would you like to be?

When they tell you –

Because you can stay just that age forever.

Will you choose her?

Or me?

Or you.

…

We have to go back now.

I know.

…

Okay. Here's what comes next:

We are eighty-three.

Seventy.

Sixty-something.

Fifty-two.

Around forty.

We're thirty-two, then twenty-one, then –

Eighteen – and ten, and six.

And further now.

(*A breath.*)

(*Simultaneous with the below.*) *We are five.*

We are five.

— — —

We have been brought to the beach today as a treat. We are not allowed into the water because they're not sure who of us can swim but the boys run down the tide line to grab slobs of wet sand which they throw at the girls, who are shrieking and running away but, so, never out of the line of fire so I know they like it really. (When I get older I'll understand how problematic this all is but on this day I am pleased that I am able to identify the rules of this particular game.)

It is incredibly beautiful and even though the sun makes my eyes hurt I think I must be quite happy, you know, from my five-year-old perspective I guess I assume I am – 'happy'. There are some clouds of course but the sky is flat and warm and the sea smells salty and huge just like I knew it would and the sand feels like sugar but does not taste like it.

There are a lot of real families around us and they're doing things like paddling tiny ones or flinging each other up and out of the sea to tangle-splash back down and they have this kind of special laughter that makes my mouth water.

The people who look after us are sitting on blankets and they're wearing sunglasses and no one can tell who they're looking at but I know they're not looking at me because they never do look at me. I don't know why it would be any different at the beach than at the home.

I'm thinking about the playground that I saw by the car park when we got off the bus. I'm thinking about the swings in the playground, and look, I really love swings, so I make my way back to the playground because no one really notices where I go or what I do anyway. But when I get there, there are some big girls on the swings and I desperately want them to see me and ask me over to play with them. But I wait around for ages and, you know, duh, those big girls don't notice me either.

There are these bars in the playground – not monkey-bars, not high, sort of come up to my chest when I'm standing up, not dangerous. I'm not sure what they're for but I think they look like quite good things for hanging upside down on, so I get my,

my knees over the bar and so I am – if you can picture it –
looking down into the sky and I see –

Um.

Looking down there now into the sky and suddenly

it

curves, I see it is actually a curve underneath me like a dish,
you know, sortof salad bowl, not the simple flat backdrop to the
small events of my little life I have taken it to be before.

And I look at it for so long that it, I don't know if it rewires
something? But for so long anyway that I spose I faint, I know
I feel fizzing in my head and my cheeks prickling from all the
blood there but I can't stop looking because I understand
something that no one else does. And it terrifies me.

I think I've found some secret out about the world. Or that she
is sharing her secret with me – because, being five, how am I to
know people have been hanging around the wrong way up and
looking down into the great blue bowl of the sky for thousands
of years.

The last thing I remember before I faint is one of the care
workers running towards me shouting about how I am showing
my knickers and that all the boys are looking and don't I have
any shame? And then the ground, as they say, rushes up to meet
me, the *thwunk* my small body makes against it somehow a
comfort after the cold cold forever of the sky.

After I come to, and right side up, I can still see the curve.
Something in me has opened right up, and at the same moment,
there is this lid there that hasn't been there before. Like I am the
spider under the glass now. And all I can see is the great hot
weight of the sky and the rest of my life pressing and tightening
and squashing me down until I am dead.

…

Did you hear her?

I hear her.

That was us.

Yes.

That was the moment she found out about us.

I kept it.

— — —

Were we happy, ever? After that.

Enough. As much as anyone.

A little lonelier perhaps.

But.

Maybe we should have stayed the wrong way up.

Maybe we did?

Ha.

I'm sorry I didn't believe that you would ever happen to me.

…

Do you remember before, when I promised you nothing bad would happen to you?

How could I have promised you that? You must have known it was a lie. Maybe you wanted to believe me for a moment, but you knew there's no way I could promise you something like that.

Even though, maybe, you would like to be told, you would like to hear and to taste just for a moment and be held for a moment by –

I'll keep you safe.

Nothing bad is going to happen to you.

Nobody ever said that to me.

I wonder is it too late now.

…

Hello, little one. Hello. I'm talking to you.

Just – try to believe me:

Nothing bad is going to happen to you. Not while I'm here.

You're

Safe.

Promise?

…

Yes.

We're all here now, the three parts of you. Still beating heart and breathing lungs and believing believing belie–

…

…

Getting old.

Talking to myself.

I'll start again.

End.

www.nickhernbooks.co.uk

facebook.com/nickhernbooks

twitter.com/nickhernbooks